Spouse ABUSE

Assessing & Treating Battered Women, Batterers, & Their Children

Second Edition

Michele Harway, PhD, ABPP
Marsali Hansen, PhD, ABPP

Professional Resource Press
Sarasota, Florida

A 6-credit home study continuing education program is available as a supplement to this book. See last page for additional information.

Published by
Professional Resource Press
(An imprint of the Professional Resource Exchange, Inc.)
Post Office Box 15560
Sarasota, FL 34277-1560

Printed in the United States of America

This publication is sold with the understanding that the publisher is not engaged in rendering professional services. If legal, psychological, medical, accounting, or other expert advice or assistance is sought or required, the reader should seek the services of a competent professional.

The copy editor for this book was Patricia Rockwood, the managing editor was Debbie Fink, the production coordinator was Laurie Girsch, and the cover designer was Jami Stinnet.

Library of Congress Cataloging-in-Publication Data

Harway, Michele.
    Spouse abuse : assessing & treating battered women, batterers, & their children / Michele Harway, Marsali Hansen.-- 2nd ed.
        p. cm.
    Includes bibliographical references and index.
    ISBN 1-56887-085-X (alk. paper)
    1. Wife abuse. 2. Abusive men--Rehabilitation. 3. Abused wives--Rehabilitation. 4. Children of abused wives--Rehabilitation. I. Hansen, Marsali. II. Title.

RC569.5.F3H37 2004
616.85'822--dc22

2003062664

Acknowledgments

I would like to give special thanks to the individuals who assisted with this manuscript, especially Jodi Miciak, Harriet Bicksler, and Jason Weller. Particular thanks go to the individuals whose passion, encouragement, and commitment to the topic would not let me rest until we revisited this book again: Toni Dupont-Morales, Helen Hendy, and Pamela Shirey.

Marsali Hansen, 2004

With this revision, I am greatly indebted to my colleague Kendall Evans for his influence on my thinking especially as it relates to working with the batterer. Thanks also to Ola Barnett for her willingness to share resources with us as we revised. I also want to acknowledge the work of my colleagues on the Interdivisional Grant Project on Intimate Partner Abuse and Relationship Violence (funded by CODAPAR of the American Psychological Association): Robert Geffner, David Ivey, Mary P. Koss, Bianca Cody Murphy, Jeffery Scott Mio, and James M. O'Neil.

Michele Harway, 2004

Our publisher, Larry Ritt, deserves a big thank you from both of us for encouraging us to prepare this revision for a second edition.

Michele Harway and Marsali Hansen, 2004

Preface to the
Second Edition

In the 11 years which have elapsed since the publication of the first edition of this book, there has been a virtual proliferation of books on the subject of spousal abuse. Most have focused on the expanding empirical base on this topic. Nonetheless, clinicians' knowledge about how to assess and intervene with individuals and families touched by this social problem remains scanty. Fortunately, in some jurisdictions, public recognition of the prevalence and seriousness of violence in families has led to calls for better training for mental health professionals. Several states now mandate domestic violence training in graduate programs and continuing education for licensed clinicians. We are hopeful that soon all clinicians will have the skills necessary to help affected families. In the meantime, we offer an expanded version of our earlier book. This book continues to be of immediate utility as it provides hands-on training for clinicians at a variety of levels.

Since the publication of the earlier edition, terms such as domestic violence and intimate partner violence have been more frequently used than "spousal abuse." Some have objected to the use of "spousal abuse" as implying that violence occurs only within the context of a marital relationship. However, the term "spouse" itself has been more broadly applied in the last 11 years so that it is now understood to apply not only to married couples but also to other couples in committed relationships, whether heterosexual or homosexual. At the same time, we recognize that dating couples also experience a great deal of violence and much of what we describe in this book applies equally to dating couples. Although we refer primarily to spousal abuse throughout the book, we also use other terms such as domestic violence, intimate partner violence, and other closely related terms.

This edition reports up-to-date information about the prevalence and seriousness of spousal abuse. We have expanded the information about how to conduct an assessment, revised and elaborated on how to work with batterers, and have greatly expanded the sections on assessing and treating children. We remain convinced that families exposed to violence are affected at multiple levels and therefore believe that intervention must also occur at multiple levels. We are dedicated to seeing all clinicians develop minimum levels of competency for work with families affected by violence.

Table of Contents

Spouse ABUSE

Assessing & Treating Battered Women, Batterers, & Their Children

Second Edition

1

What Kinds of
Families Are Violent?

HOW COMMON
IS VIOLENCE IN THE FAMILY?

"The American family and the American home are perhaps as or more violent than any other single American institution or setting. . . . Americans run the greatest risks of assault, physical injury, and even murder in their own homes by members of their own families" (Straus, Gelles, & Steinmetz, 1980, p. 4). Shocking as it may be, this statement tells us something about the prevalence of familial violence in our society. And, although this quotation is more than 20 years old, it is as relevant today as when it first appeared in print. In support of this statement, Greenfeld et al. (1998) indicate that 3 out of 4 victims of intimate violence included in official government statistics were assaulted in their homes.

We present these findings here to convince our readers of the necessity of learning about how to treat spousal abuse and each person affected by it.* No longer can clinicians assume that only specialists in domestic violence must be knowledgeable about this problem. In fact, it is highly likely that all practitioners will at some point be treating either a violent individual, the target of that violence, or a child who views the violence. Every clinician, therefore, must be an expert in the assessment and treatment of spousal abuse. It is our intention, with this book, to provide the information necessary to sensitize clinicians to the issue and to outline treatment strategies and interventions.

It is difficult for clinicians with no personal experience of spousal abuse to understand its insidiousness. "Case Example 1" (pp. 8-10) presents a family in which spousal abuse follows a typical course.

---

*Spousal abuse is also referred to as domestic violence or intimate partner violence.

Statistics about the prevalence of spousal abuse differ for a variety of methodological reasons, such as how violence is defined or measured, who is surveyed, and the context of the study (e.g., when spousal abuse is assessed as part of a study of crime, prevalence statistics are somewhat lower because most do not think of domestic violence as a crime, even though it is). Some of the commonly reported figures are those of Gelles and Straus (1989), which indicate that 1 out of every 6 wives reports that she has been hit by her husband at some point in her marriage.* In 6 cases out of 1,000 the attack takes the form of a severe beating, and in 2 cases out of 1,000 the attack involves the use of guns or knives. More recent figures support earlier findings with 1 out of 5 women reporting being assaulted by an intimate partner (Tjaden & Thoennes, 1998).

Estimates were made that 8.7 million couples experienced at least one assault during 1985 (Straus & Gelles, 1988). The same researchers estimate that in 3.4 million households, the violence had a relatively high risk of causing injury. More recently, Tjaden and Thoennes (1998) indicated that there are 9 million incidents of spousal abuse annually. These figures must be taken with some caution because experts estimate that the actual figures are likely to be considerably higher. There is widespread agreement that reports of incidents of spousal abuse far underestimate actual figures (Kilpatrick, Edwards, & Seymour, 1992; Tjaden & Thoennes, 1998, 2000). Greenfeld et al. (1998) estimate that only about half of the women who experience violence perpetrated by an intimate report it to the police. And it is not only the couple who are impacted by spousal abuse, but also the children in the household. It is estimated that 3.3 million to 10 million children are exposed to spousal abuse (Carlson, 1984; Straus, 1991). The National Crime Victimization Survey indicates that children under 12 live in more than half of the households where women are physically abused (Greenfeld et al., 1998). Moreover, as many as 30% to 70% of batterers are reported to abuse their children as well (Hughes, 1982; Pagelow, 1989; Straus et al., 1980).

Of course, spousal abuse is not restricted to couples who are legally married. Koss (1990) indicates that the proportion of violence in dating relationships is extremely high – fully 50% of couples have experienced it. Dating violence is said to affect 10% of high school students (Silverman et al., 2001) and from 22% (Sorenson & Bowie, 1994) to 39% of college students (White & Koss, 1991). Likewise, violence is not something unique to heterosexual couples: Renzetti (1993) found that as many as

---

*Because 95% of batterers are men and most of the battered are women (Connors & Harway, 1995), the male pronoun will be used throughout this book to refer to batterers and the female pronoun will refer to those battered.

59% of lesbian couples have also experienced violence. In one of the few studies of gay male violence, 17% of gay men surveyed reported having been in a physically violent relationship (Gay and Lesbian Community Action Council, 1987). Looking at a variety of published studies, the National Coalition of Anti-Violence Programs (1997) concluded that as many as 25% to 33% of gay and lesbian relationships included violence. Likewise, spousal abuse is found in all groups regardless of socioeconomic status, religion, or racial/ethnic background. For example, Tjaden and Thoennes (2000) report that Hispanic and non-Hispanic women are equally likely to experience physical assault and stalking victimization. Bachman and Saltzman (1995) report similar figures of spousal abuse across a number of ethnic groups. Greenfeld et al. (1998), however, indicate that spousal abuse is higher among black women aged 16 to 24, women in the lowest income groups, and those living in urban areas.

These statistics clearly indicate that spousal abuse is a problem that affects people from a wide variety of backgrounds.

HOW SERIOUS IS SPOUSAL VIOLENCE?

Some practitioners, aware of the incidence of violence today, are not aware of the seriousness of violent episodes and thus tend to underestimate the danger their clients may experience.

Yet, the research indicates that conjugal assaults tend to have serious consequences. About half of victims of spousal abuse reported a physical injury (Greenfeld et al., 1998). About 50% of those injuries were relatively minor (bruises and similar trauma); the remainder were relatively serious, and many of those were injuries to the head or face. About 30% of female victims were killed by an intimate, a figure that remained the same as in 1976 (Greenfeld et al., 1998).

A study of 300 shelter residents indicates that these women had endured an average of 59 assaults each. Prior to intake, each woman had on the average experienced over five assaults every 4 weeks, for an annualized frequency rate of over 65 conjugal assaults per year. Over 20% stated that they were being assaulted twice or more per week. Sixty-two percent of women who had ever been pregnant during their abusive relationships had been assaulted during a pregnancy. Two-thirds of the sample had experienced at least one assault where they were extensively beaten up or worse. One in 6 had been threatened with a knife or gun by her partner, and one in 30 had actually been attacked with a knife or gun (Okun, 1986). These 300 women reported on intake 28 fractures (most commonly of the nose or jaw) and 22 serious injuries not involving fractures (chronic back injuries, torn ligaments, dislocations, ruptured eardrums, broken teeth, lacerations, stab wounds, bullet wounds). These injuries included only those that had been sustained at the time of intake, not previous injuries.

A frightening finding is that of this group, only 24% of women had ever received medical treatment for injuries sustained during conjugal assaults. The remainder had wanted medical treatment but were prevented by their partner from obtaining it. Sixty-nine percent of these women had experienced at least one assault that resulted in police intervention, and over 17% had received multiple visits from the police. Similarly, Greenfeld et al. (1998) report that only 1 in 10 women victimized by an intimate other had sought medical treatment. However, in 1994 (Greenfeld et al., 1998) there were more than a quarter of a million hospital visits resulting from spousal abuse, and there are annually $150 million dollars in medical expenses accrued.

In many cases, domestic violence results in murder, with lethality in cases of wife battering most likely to occur when the woman tries to leave (Browne, 1987). That women are in particular danger is substantiated by the finding that almost a third of female murder victims are killed by a husband, an ex-husband, or a nonmarital partner (Greenfeld et al., 1998).

Thus, serious injury (or death) as a result of domestic violence is highly likely. In addition to injuries or death to the recipients of domestic violence, children who witness spousal abuse experience damage both over the short and the long term; and symptoms may range from internalizing problems to externalizing problems (Barnett, Miller-Perrin, & Perrin, 1997).

CONTEXT WITHIN WHICH
BATTERING OCCURS

Understanding spousal abuse requires an understanding of the cultural context within which battering occurs. "Men who assault their wives are actually living up to cultural prescriptions that are cherished in Western society – aggressiveness, male dominance, and female subordination – and they are using physical force as a means to enforce that dominance" (R. E. Dobash & R. P. Dobash, 1979, p. 24).

Sex-role stereotypes may maintain battering as the societal problem that it is today. In fact, a number of researchers, studying the causal pathways for a variety of types of violence, attribute violence to gender-role conflict and hyper-masculinity (Connors & Harway, 1995; Lisak & Roth, 1988; O'Neil & Egan, 1993; O'Neil & Nadeau, 1999; Pryor, 1992). Another explanation is that the traditional family is a system where the balance of power is inherently unequal, mimicking other relationships of men and women, where men have usually held the power and women have been subservient to those in power over them. One of the effects of power imbalance is that women, as the less powerful member of the family, learn to be more accommodating and also to tune in more to the needs of their spouse. This pattern of behavior is accentuated among battered women, as evidenced by the complacency that many battered women exhibit, their difficulties in leaving, and the tendency to placate the batterer so as to avoid repetition of violent episodes (Nutt, 1999). Other research substantiates that females are more emotionally expressive than males. Thus women are seen as being emotional (equated with irrationality) and men as nonexpressive (equated with rationality). At the same time, expressions of aggressiveness (which is more characteristic of males) are not typically labeled as expressions of emotion nor as irrational acts.

Expressions of aggression by a batterer toward his wife (even those stemming from a loss of control) fail to be condemned by society because they are role congruent, whereas fighting back (usually in self-defense) by the wife would be condemned because it is incongruent with the female gender-role.

WHO SEEKS TREATMENT?

We have argued that the statistics cited previously suggest that at some point in their practice all therapists will find in their waiting room either a battered woman, a batterer, the children of these couples, or someone else affected by spousal violence. Thus, it is important to know exactly how these individuals will present when they seek treatment.

Will they come for therapy to rid themselves of the violence? Some research suggests otherwise. Holtzworth-Munroe et al. (1992) describe their efforts to find a nonviolent control group for a study of spousal violence. In five different studies, they sought nonviolent maritally distressed couples from psychological and family therapy clinics and nonviolent nondistressed couples from the surrounding community. Among the maritally distressed but allegedly nonviolent couples, 55% to 56% of the men actually reported having at some time engaged in violent behavior toward their wives and their therapists did not know about the violence. Among the nondistressed couples, 30% to 34% of the men (depending on the sample) were violent toward their wives.

In the same study, the percent of husbands who had been violent toward their wives in the previous year ranged from 43% to 46% (depending on the sample) among the distressed couples and 15% to 21% among the nondistressed couples. Although the majority of the violent behaviors were not classified as severe (but did include pushing, grabbing, shoving, throwing things, and slapping), husbands had generally engaged in several different violent behaviors and/or in one violent behavior more than once. Some husbands had engaged in severe violent behaviors such as choking or using a knife or gun.

The Holtzworth-Munroe et al. (1992) study suggests that a critical skill for clinicians, therefore, must be assessment for spousal abuse. In Chapter 3, we will describe how this assessment should be conducted.

One final note: Our interest in this area was motivated by some research we conducted (Hansen, Harway, & Cervantes, 1991; Harway & Hansen, 1993a, 1993b) suggesting that even experienced therapists were not knowledgeable in assessing or treating spousal violence. In both studies, therapists received a questionnaire by mail that mentioned a case vignette of an actual violent family. In the first study, therapists were members of the American Association of Marriage and Family Therapy (AAMFT) and included both master's and doctoral level clinicians representing themselves as marriage counselors, clinical social workers, psychologists, and psychiatrists. After the presentation of the vignette, they were asked to describe what was happening in the family, what interventions they would make, what outcome they would expect from their intervention, and what legal and ethical issues the case raises. When asked to describe what was going on in this case, 40% of practitioners in this sample failed to address the issue of violence (even though the violence was clear in the case). Moreover, among those identifying the conflict, the severity was minimized: Ninety-one percent of those who addressed the conflict considered it mild or moderate.

Recognition of family violence is an important first step, but no less important are the therapists' descriptions of how they would intervene. Because even those who addressed the violence underplayed its seriousness, the interventions they subsequently recommended were inappropriate. Fully 55% of respondents *would not* intervene as if the violence required any immediate action. The results were consistent across characteristics of the respondent (master's or doctoral education, psychologist or other license, and gender). There were few differences by theoretical orientation of the respondent.

The second study also involved a mail questionnaire, this time sent to a random sample of the memberships of several practice divisions of the American Psychological Association (APA; Divisions 12 [Clinical Psychology], 29 [Psychotherapy], and 42 [Independent Practice]). A case in which rather extreme domestic violence was implicated was presented to respondents.

Results of the second study supported those of Study 1 in that some substantial proportion of our psychologist respondents did not generate appropriate interventions even when told outright that the case was one of domestic violence with a lethal outcome.

The fact that relatively consistent findings were obtained from both studies suggests that many psychotherapists (with a variety of types of training) are unable to formulate appropriate intervention plans even when explicitly told that a case is a violent one. Moreover, it also appears that therapists are unprepared to assess for dangerousness in violent families. In the second study, diagnoses given by respondents prior to knowing about the homicide were compared to assessments of dynamics made after being told that the case had resulted in a murder. Diagnoses and assessments were remarkably similar: A substantial proportion of respondents used as a diagnosis a V code for marital problems (V61.10 in *DSM-III-R* [American Psychiatric Association, 1987] which corresponds to V61.1 in *DSM-IV* [American Psychiatric Association, 1994]). After being told that a murder had occurred, most still speculated that the underlying dynamics of the case were heavily dependent on the couple's issues. Only a handful of respondents, either before learning of the homicide or after, focused on the pathology of the perpetrator! Moreover, fully one-half of our sample, asked what intervention they could have made prior to the fatal outcome, failed to consider obtaining protection for the wife or of insuring her safety.

WORKING WITH FAMILIES
EXPERIENCING SPOUSAL ABUSE

The data presented in this section make it clear that working with families that experience spousal abuse is difficult work, fraught with peril both for the clients and the therapist. Because of the prevalence of spousal abuse and the danger that clients are in, mental health professionals are cautioned to be knowledgeable about this issue, competent in assessment and treatment of violent families, and willing to consider the possibility of abuse even when the clients present with problems seemingly unrelated to violence. Moreover, the impact on the children must also be considered, whether or not the parents are aware of their child's exposure.

Case Example 1:
Susan and George*

Susan Spence met George Gambrills at a church social. From the first, she was quite taken by him: tall, good-looking, very personable, gainfully employed as an engineer at an aircraft manufacturer, and with all the characteristics of a potential marriage partner. George perceived Susan as the woman of his dreams: intelligent, moral, financially able to contribute to a family, and very beautiful. They dated for 8 months. Their courtship was idyllic: George was very romantic; he frequently bought her roses and gifts and took her to expensive restaurants. He enjoyed being with her so much that they spent virtually all of their time together. Susan began to distance herself somewhat from her girlfriends. For one, she had little time left after work that was not spent with George. Also, George had reasons for not liking each of her friends, and she began to feel alienated from the individuals themselves. George found himself suspicious of Susan's friends. He felt she should need him and come to him instead, claiming that was what a relationship was supposed to be. By the time he proposed, George was her best and only friend. Susan immediately said yes and began preparing for the wedding. George was intricately involved in the planning. He wanted a fancy white-tie wedding. He wanted a Saturday night wedding at a big hotel in town. He wanted beef Wellington for the main course. He wanted his brother Fred to be best man and his sister Erica to be maid of honor. He said he felt uncomfortable with Susan's brother Tom and did not want him to be an attendant. He wanted his cousins Samantha and Benjamin to be attendants. Susan had dreamed of her wedding for many years. George's plans were very different from the wedding she had envisioned. Though Susan was upset, she was so in love that she acquiesced to all of his requests.

---

*Names and all identifying characteristics of persons in all case examples have been disguised thoroughly to protect privacy. None of these persons or cases refer to any specific client; all are composites drawn from numerous cases.

Shortly after the wedding, George seemed to change and began to be abusive. At first he simply put her down. She wasn't as perfect as he thought she was, but then she had never been married before, and with a little instruction. . . . His criticisms increased to nagging and deriding her, expressing unfounded jealousy, and spewing insults about her family and workmates. Then he began insisting she restrict her activities, forbidding her to leave the house during her time off, controlling the family finances, and eventually complaining so much about her work that she quit her job. Susan felt relief at quitting her job, as shortly thereafter she discovered she was pregnant. Relationships with her family began to deteriorate because George began to tell her things that relatives had allegedly said about her behind her back. Susan was upset when George forbade her mother staying with her when her baby, George, Jr., was born. However, she thought George would be kinder now that he had the son he had always wanted. Instead, George, Sr., found fault with everything she did for the child. In addition, he did not help with the care of the baby, but would hold him and tell him how inept his mother was. George felt Susan let herself go physically after the birth of the baby and was angry that she no longer looked like the woman he married.

The first time that George struck her, Susan was stunned. He had been yelling at her about her slovenly housekeeping and how poorly she was caring for the child when suddenly he pushed her so hard she fell over the coffee table. He also punched her so hard in the face that her ponytails came undone. The morning following the fight, George was contrite, telling her that he had so much pressure at work that he had lost his mind. He apologized and bought her an exquisite bracelet to make up for hurting her. He promised that it would never happen again.

Unfortunately, the violence continued and became more and more acute and more and more frequent, each time followed by a period of contriteness with George going out of his way to be especially loving to atone for his loss of control. Most of the time, George would slam Susan against the wall, once even going so far as to slam her so severely that her hearing was affected. At other times, George would become enraged and lock her in the apartment, leaving her isolated for days at a time. Young George, Jr., was watching his father. At the age of 2 he would become aggressive toward other children, biting them and kicking them. Throughout it all, Susan continued to love George, excusing his violence by pointing to the extreme stress of his job and indicating that the real George was the loving man who bought her gifts and acted so lovingly following a fight. She also felt her young son was only going through a "stage" and would learn to behave better.

Susan became pregnant with Caitie when George, Jr., was 4. Her husband was angry and complained that they did not have the money for another child. He did not accompany her to the hospital for the birth of their daughter. When Caitie was a baby her father refused to have anything to do with her. He began to belittle her just like he belittled Susan. When Caitie was 4 she began to complain of headaches. Her pediatrician recognized these as stress related and recommended the family seek counseling. George, Jr., continued to have difficulty in situations where he was required to accommodate other children. He was very disruptive and impulsive in preschool. Susan was addressing the concerns of George, Jr.'s preschool teacher and Caitie's pediatrician when she sought out psychotherapy.

2

How Much Do You Know About Spousal Abuse?

Before continuing with other chapters, readers may want to complete this self-quiz to assess their current knowledge about spousal abuse. The first section of this chapter begins with the self-quiz, continues with answers to the quiz, and concludes with detailed information relating to each correct answer. The self-quiz is an important adjunct to training in this area, because our research (Hansen et al., 1991; Harway & Hansen, 1993a, 1993b) indicates that clinicians feel ill-equipped to intervene with this population. It is likely that the many myths about spousal violence have been accepted as truth by psychotherapists as well as others. The self-quiz was developed for this book based in part on myths about domestic violence in Lenore Walker's (1979) book *The Battered Woman* and in the New Jersey Domestic Violence Model Curriculum.

SELF-QUIZ

Indicate whether each statement is True (T) or False (F):

_____   1.   Battered women represent only a small percentage of the population.

_____   2.   A man who verbally intimidates or harasses his partner is *not* likely to lash out physically.

_____   3.   Research indicates that battered women are masochistic.

_____   4.   Violence in the home rarely results in *serious* injuries or permanent damage.

_____   5.   Unlike poorer women, middle-class women are not likely to get battered.

_____   6.   Twenty percent of all Americans approve of hitting a spouse on appropriate occasions.

_____   7.   Minority women are battered more frequently than Anglo women.

_____   8.   Women who repeatedly leave and return to violent partners do so *mainly* because they are emotionally unable to separate from them.

_____   9.   Religious beliefs strongly decrease the probability of becoming a batterer.

_____   10. If spouse abuse is suspected, mental health professionals are required by law to report it to the authorities.

_____   11. Battered women are uneducated and have few job skills.

_____   12. Alcohol causes battering when the man drinks.

_____   13. Batterers are violent in all their relationships.

_____   14. Batterers are unsuccessful and lack resources to cope with the world.

_____ 15. The most important goal in working with a battered woman is to help her leave the abusive partner.

_____ 16. Battering is the single major cause of injuries to women, more than stranger rapes, muggings, and automobile accidents combined.

_____ 17. Batterers have psychopathic personalities.

_____ 18. In most parts of the country, police have been unsuccessful in protecting a battered woman.

_____ 19. It would be appropriate to think of a battered woman as a hostage in her own home.

_____ 20. A woman's nagging is a major cause of violence in the home.

_____ 21. The batterer is not a loving partner.

_____ 22. A wife batterer also beats his children.

_____ 23. Pregnant women tend to be "immune" to assaults by their partners during the course of their pregnancies.

_____ 24. Once a battered woman, always a battered woman.

_____ 25. Once a batterer, always a batterer.

_____ 26. Threats to turn in a woman to immigration, welfare, or other authorities are considered domestic violence, in that they represent the batterer's efforts to control his partner.

_____ 27. Some women deserve to be beaten.

_____ 28. The diagnostic clue "accident prone" may appear in the history of some women.

_____ 29. Battered women can always leave home.

_____ 30. Batterers will cease their violence once the couple gets married.

_____ 31. In a battering relationship, often the batterer spontaneously stops being violent permanently, if he is happier.

_____ 32. Children need their father even if he is violent.

_____ 33. It is relatively easy to assess by her personality type whether a woman is likely to be in a battering relationship.

_____ 34. When a woman leaves an abusive relationship, the likelihood of serious injury increases.

_____ 35. The majority of battered women have been hit 1 to 3 times by their partner before being successfully helped.

_____ 36. Many battered women do things that, though unintentional, cause their husbands to hit them.

_____ 37. Signs that a partner will become a batterer are usually present during the first few weeks of the relationship.

_____ 38. Upon hearing that a woman is in an abusive relationship, the majority of mental health professionals are most concerned about the woman's safety.

_____ 39. The majority of abused senior citizens are beaten by their partners.

_____ 40. Battering usually occurs when the husband's feelings of love for his partner are replaced by anger and hate.

_____ 41. Most children who live in violent homes are unaware of the violence.

_____ 42. Couples who experience domestic violence and who seek counseling will usually tell their counselor about the violence.

_____ 43. Working on relationship issues in couple's therapy will help increase the violence.

_____ 44. Most women would rather experience psychological abuse than physical abuse.

_____ 45. Children acquire the characteristics of their abusive fathers by copying his aggression.

_____ 46. Spouse abuse has no long-term impact on children, and once out of the abusive environment children recover without intervention.

SELF-QUIZ ANSWERS

Let us see how you did:

_F_   1. Battered women represent only a small percentage of the population.

_F_   2. A man who verbally intimidates or harasses his partner is *not* likely to lash out physically.

_F_   3. Research indicates that battered women are masochistic.

_F_   4. Violence in the home rarely results in *serious* injuries or permanent damage.

_F_   5. Unlike poorer women, middle-class women are not likely to get battered.

_T_   6. Twenty percent of all Americans approve of hitting a spouse on appropriate occasions.

_F_   7. Minority women are battered more frequently than Anglo women.

_F_   8. Women who repeatedly leave and return to violent partners do so *mainly* because they are emotionally unable to separate from them.

_F_   9. Religious beliefs strongly decrease the probability of becoming a batterer.

_F_   10. If spouse abuse is suspected, mental health professionals are required by law to report it to the authorities.

_F_   11. Battered women are uneducated and have few job skills.

_F_   12. Alcohol causes battering when the man drinks.

_T/F_   13. Batterers are violent in all their relationships.

_F_   14. Batterers are unsuccessful and lack resources to cope with the world.

___F___ 15. The most important goal in working with a battered woman is to help her leave the abusive partner.

___T___ 16. Battering is the single major cause of injuries to women, more than stranger rapes, muggings, and automobile accidents combined.

___F___ 17. Batterers have psychopathic personalities.

___T___ 18. In most parts of the country, police have been unsuccessful in protecting a battered woman.

___T___ 19. It would be appropriate to think of a battered woman as a hostage in her own home.

___F___ 20. A woman's nagging is a major cause of violence in the home.

___F___ 21. The batterer is not a loving partner.

___T/F___ 22. A wife batterer also beats his children.

___F___ 23. Pregnant women tend to be "immune" to assaults by their partners during the course of their pregnancies.

___F___ 24. Once a battered woman, always a battered woman.

___T___ 25. Once a batterer, always a batterer.

___T___ 26. Threats to turn in a woman to immigration, welfare, or other authorities are considered domestic violence, in that they represent the batterer's efforts to control his partner.

___F___ 27. Some women deserve to be beaten.

___T___ 28. The diagnostic clue "accident prone" may appear in the history of some women.

___F___ 29. Battered women can always leave home.

___F___ 30. Batterers will cease their violence once the couple gets married.

___F___   31.   In a battering relationship, often the batterer spontaneously stops being violent permanently, if he is happier.

___F___   32.   Children need their father even if he is violent.

___F___   33.   It is relatively easy to assess by her personality type whether a woman is likely to be in a battering relationship.

___T___   34.   When a woman leaves an abusive relationship, the likelihood of serious injury increases.

___F___   35.   The majority of battered women have been hit 1 to 3 times by their partner before being successfully helped.

___F___   36.   Many battered women do things that, though unintentional, cause their husbands to hit them.

___F___   37.   Signs that a partner will become a batterer are usually present during the first few weeks of the relationship.

___F___   38.   Upon hearing that a woman is in an abusive relationship, the majority of mental health professionals are most concerned about the woman's safety.

___T___   39.   The majority of abused senior citizens are beaten by their partners.

___F___   40.   Battering usually occurs when the husband's feelings of love for his partner are replaced by anger and hate.

___F___   41.   Most children who live in violent homes are unaware of the violence.

___F___   42.   Couples who experience domestic violence and who seek counseling will usually tell their counselor about the violence.

___T___   43.   Working on relationship issues in couple's therapy will help increase the violence.

___F___   44.   Most women would rather experience psychological abuse than physical abuse.

__F__   45. Children acquire the characteristics of their abusive fathers by copying his aggression.

__F__   46. Spouse abuse has no long-term impact on children, and once out of the abusive environment children recover without intervention.

DETAILED ANSWERS

Now for a detailed explanation of the answers on the self-quiz. These detailed answers are organized by topic rather than chronologically. Thus, those statements that refer to general issues regarding physical or psychological violence are presented in the first section. Items relating to the prevalence and seriousness of spousal abuse follow. Myths about violence are followed by the effect on children, cultural issues about battering, and the dynamics of battering. The chapter concludes with a discussion about assessment and treatment issues, couple's therapy, and legal and ethical concerns.

PHYSICAL OR PSYCHOLOGICAL VIOLENCE

Statement 2:   *A man who verbally intimidates or harasses his partner is NOT likely to lash out physically.*

This statement is FALSE. Experts on battering agree that physical violence is at one end of the spectrum but that verbal intimidation, harassment, and similar actions represent escalating attempts to control the partner (Walker, 1979). Ultimately these behaviors will lead to physical violence.

***

Statement 19:   *It would be appropriate to think of a battered woman as a hostage in her own home.*

Statement 26:   *Threats to turn in a woman to immigration, welfare, or other authorities are considered domestic violence, in that they represent the batterer's efforts to control his partner.*

These statements are TRUE. The escalating violence and control exerted by a batterer includes social isolation of the victim and the severing of her ties with friends and family as a way to get her under his control (Walker, 1984). Eventually, the woman may very much become a hostage in her own home, powerless to leave and frightened for her survival. Threats to turn her in to the authorities also represent ways that the batterer exerts his control over his woman.

PREVALENCE AND SERIOUSNESS

Statement 1:   **Battered women represent only a small percentage of the population.**

This statement is FALSE. Depending on which statistic you consult (and they vary based on definitions of battering and samples selected), anywhere from 3.8 million to 8.7 million couples experience violence. Koss (1990) indicates that 28% to 33% of married couples experience violence at some point during their relationship. Dating violence is also quite common; Koss indicates that as many as 50% of dating couples experience violence. And battering is not restricted to heterosexual couples: Renzetti (1993) reports that as many as 59% of lesbians are in battering relationships. Regardless of which figure you decide to heed, battering affects a substantial proportion of the population.

Statement 4:   **Violence in the home rarely results in SERIOUS injuries or permanent damage.**

This statement is FALSE, too (Okun, 1986).

Statement 16:   **Battering is the single major cause of injuries to women, more than stranger rapes, muggings, and automobile accidents combined.**

This statement is TRUE. In addition, battering can be lethal. Greenfeld et al.'s (1998) data indicate that almost a third of female murder victims are killed by a husband, an ex-husband, or a nonmarital partner. For this reason, any report of violence in the home must always be taken very seriously by the clinician.

MYTHS ABOUT VIOLENCE

Statement 3:   **Research indicates that battered women are masochistic.**

Statement 33:   **It is relatively easy to assess by her personality type whether a woman is likely to be in a battering relationship.**

These statements are FALSE. In spite of repeated attempts to profile the predisposing factors to becoming a battered woman, no single profile has been described in the research literature. In fact, Hotaling and Sugarman (1986), examining 400 studies of battering, find that the only common trait shared by women who are battered is a slightly greater tendency than nonbattered women to come from abusive families. Nor has a single study indicated that battered women are likely to be any more masochistic than other women, or to share any other personality constellation with other battered women. In fact, Follingstad, Neckerman, and Vormbrock (1988) have indicated that the symptoms that battered women present in therapy are almost certain to be the *result* of years of battering rather than to provide a causal explanation as to who will be battered.

Statement 8:   *Women who repeatedly leave and return to violent part-ners do so MAINLY because they are emotionally un-able to separate from them.*

Statement 29:   *Battered women can always leave home.*

These statements are FALSE. Statistics indicate that battered women leave their batterers more frequently than has been believed. Browne (1987) indicates that battered women make an average of seven attempts to leave before they are able to do so permanently. When these women return, they almost invariably indicate that the person they went to did not take them seriously. Family members have often pushed the women to try harder. Clergy, doctors, and even psychotherapists have often urged battered women to modify their own behavior in order to effect a change in the relationship. Other times, helpers have seemingly been unaware of the physical danger the women are in. Goodstein and Page (1981), for instance, indicate that battered women who presented to a medical emergency setting report having gone to a therapist, usually for only one session, and not returning because the therapist *never even asked them about the battering.* Thus, when a battered woman leaves her batterer and seeks help from another, inability to obtain emotional support is the most common reason for returning to the abusive situation. Other reasons include lack of financial resources and fear for the safety of the children.

Statement 20: **A woman's nagging is a major cause of violence in the home.**

Statement 27: **Some women deserve to be beaten.**

Statement 36: **Many battered women do things that, though unintentional, cause their husbands to hit them.**

All of these statements are FALSE. Violence is always the responsibility of the person who commits it. Although nagging can be unpleasant, and battered women may engage in behaviors that are very disagreeable, a batterer has numerous alternatives to violence, such as leaving the room.

Statement 23: **Pregnant women tend to be "immune" to assaults by their partners during the course of their pregnancies.**

This statement is FALSE. Pregnant women who have been battered are at high risk during their pregnancy. For some women, the first incidence of battering may in fact have occurred during their pregnancy. Half of all battered women are abused during their pregnancy (Okun, 1986). The breasts, abdomen, and genitals seem to receive the greatest share of the blows. Researchers describe the high incidence of battering during pregnancy as being the result of the batterer's frustration that someone other than himself (the growing fetus) has an impact on her.

EFFECT ON CHILDREN

Statement 32: **Children need their father even if he is violent.**

This statement is FALSE. The statement is a myth that keeps many women in a dangerous relationship "for the sake of the children." Studies show that most children suffer permanent damage from viewing violence (J. S. Cummings et al., 1989). They may themselves become victimizers of others or may allow themselves to be victimized.

Statement 41: **Most children who live in violent homes are unaware of the violence.**

This statement is FALSE. Until the late 70s, the belief was that children were oblivious to the violence in their home or that it had no impact on them. Studies of battered women themselves suggest that they underestimate the exposure of their children. For example, only 25% of battered women in shelters believed that their children had been exposed to the violence (Tomkins et al., 1994). Yet, another study that focused on children's self-reports (Jenkins, Smith, & Graham, 1989) found that 71% of children living in violent homes witnessed the abuse. There is much research as well indicating that children who are exposed to marital violence sustain both short- and long-term damage to their cognitive, emotional, and interpersonal development.

Statement 45:   *Children acquire the characteristics of their abusive fathers by copying his aggression.*

This statement is FALSE. In the last 10 years, considerable research has been done on the impact of observing spouse abuse on children. Previous research focused on modeling as the major transmission process of violence between parents and children. Currently, research looks at more detailed social cognitive processes (Graham-Bermann, 1998). These include beliefs that children acquire scripts for conflict resolution from observing parents and that subsequently witnessing psychological abuse provides the script of demeaning and humiliation as a means of control (E. M. Cummings, 1998).

Statement 46:   *Spouse abuse has no long-term impact on children, and once out of the abusive environment children recover without intervention.*

This statement is FALSE. Children who witness abuse often suffer from symptoms consistent with Posttraumatic Stress Disorder. These symptoms persist if treatment isn't provided (Rossman, 1994) and can be provoked by additional reminders such as contact with the abuser, experience with arguing adults, and so on. In addition, concurrent factors such as poverty, drug abuse, and living in shelters have their own impact on children's functioning.

CULTURAL ISSUES

Statement 5: *Unlike poorer women, middle-class women are not likely to get battered.*

Statement 7: *Minority women are battered more frequently than Anglo women.*

Statement 11: *Battered women are uneducated and have few job skills.*

These statements are all FALSE. Most studies indicate that battering occurs across socioeconomic, racial, ethnic, and educational levels. A battered woman is everywoman. She may come from any walk of life and is as likely to be a successful professional woman as a ghetto dweller (Gelles & Straus, 1989). It is certainly the case, however, that poorer women who are battered are more likely to come to the attention of the authorities than are wealthier women. For one thing, a battering incident happening to a woman who lives in a poorly built apartment with thin walls is more likely to be heard by neighbors than is the beating received by a woman whose closest neighbor lives in the mansion a mile down the road.

Statement 9: *Religious beliefs strongly decrease the probability of becoming a batterer.*

This statement is also FALSE. As indicated previously, battering does not discriminate; it can happen to any woman. Belonging to a certain religious group does not protect a woman from being battered or prevent a man from battering her (Gelles & Straus, 1989). Battering is just as likely to occur in Christian homes as in Jewish ones; in homes where religiosity is a big focus of the family as well as in homes where religiosity is nonexistent.

DYNAMICS OF BATTERING

Statement 12: *Alcohol causes battering when the man drinks.*

Although many batterers are also alcoholics or problem drinkers, research indicates that men who abuse alcohol tend to do most of their battering when sober (Browne, 1987; Gelles & Straus, 1989). Even when battering is done under the influence of alcohol, the alcohol cannot be blamed for the battering, even though alcoholic batterers will often blame the violence on the drinking. In fact, when these men are treated for alcoholism and cease drinking, they continue to abuse their partners unless the battering, too, is treated. Thus the preceding statement is FALSE.

Statement 6:   ***Twenty percent of all Americans approve of hitting a spouse on appropriate occasions.***

Study results indicate that the statement above is TRUE (Straus et al., 1980). An impressive segment of the American population does think that under certain circumstances it is appropriate to hit a spouse. Of course, this finding is not surprising when you consider that until late in the last century it was considered the responsibility of the husband to use corporal punishment because "It is better to punish the body and correct the soul than to damage the soul and spare the body . . . readily beat her, not in rage but out of charity and concern for her soul" (quoted in Davidson, 1978, p. 99). In fact, a commonly used colloquial expression "the rule of thumb" comes from English case law that gave a husband permission to hit his wife with a rod no wider than the width of a thumb (Hart, 1993).

Statement 13:   ***Batterers are violent in all their relationships.***

Statement 22:   ***A wife batterer also beats his children.***

These statements are TRUE and also FALSE. Most batterers are usually not violent in relationships at work or with others outside the home. However, a batterer is likely to be abusive in relationships with others. Also, although many batterers are not violent with their children, in 30% to 70% of cases in which there is spouse abuse there is also child physical or sexual abuse (Hughes, 1982; Pagelow, 1989; Straus et al., 1980).

Statement 14:   ***Batterers are unsuccessful and lack resources to cope with the world.***

Statement 17:   **Batterers have psychopathic personalities.**

These statements are FALSE. Just as researchers have been unsuccessful in developing a profile of the typical battered woman, developing a profile of the typical batterer has been difficult. All kinds of men batter, successful as well as unsuccessful men (Edleson, Eisikovits, & Guttman, 1985; Hotaling & Sugarman, 1986). Although most batterers do not demonstrate any differences from other men on personality tests, researchers have found that a subset of batterers can indeed be classified as psychopathic; however, these men are also those who have been in trouble with the law in a variety of venues.

Statement 21:   **The batterer is not a loving partner.**

Statement 40:   **Battering usually occurs when the husband's feelings of love for his partner are replaced by anger and hate.**

These statements are both FALSE. Although it may be difficult to think of someone who can beat his wife senseless as a loving partner, the reality of living with a batterer is that he can often be an extremely loving and charming partner. Some researchers have described the Dr. Jekyll and Mr. Hyde nature of the batterer (Walker, 1979). Indeed, Lenore Walker explains the changes by describing the three phases of the violence cycle. The first phase includes the build-up of tension. This is inevitably followed by the explosion of violence (Phase 2 or battering phase). The third phase has been described as the honeymoon phase when the batterer once again becomes the charming, loving man the woman fell in love with. During this phase, the batterer expresses contriteness for his outburst and often courts his partner with flowers and other romantic gestures. During this phase, the batterer appears to be a very loving partner. Throughout the cycle of violence, most batterers maintain that they continue to love their partners.

Statement 30:   **Batterers will cease their violence once the couple gets married.**

Statement 31:   **In a battering relationship, often the batterer spontaneously stops being violent permanently, if he is happier.**

Both of these statements are FALSE. If a man is violent prior to marriage, it is likely that the violence will increase once the couple gets married. Battering often escalates and needs to be treated. It is a common misconception of women who are battered that if they could only figure out how to make their mates happier (or if only his job situation got better, or if he could better control his drinking) then the violence would cease. The battering must be acknowledged as a characteristic of the batterer and not as something the woman has much control over, and in most cases, it must be treated for it to cease (Hansen & Harway, 1993).

Statement 37:   ***Signs that a partner will become a batterer are usually present in the first few weeks of the relationship.***

FALSE. There are no consistent patterns regarding when abuse first appears or how it manifests. Violence may occur early in the relationship or take some time to develop. Usually, there has been a progression of abuse from verbal to increasingly violent physical abuse over some extended period of time.

ASSESSMENT AND TREATMENT ISSUES

Statement 15:   ***The most important goal in working with a battered woman is to help her leave the abusive partner.***

This statement is FALSE. After making sure that a battered woman is safe, empowerment is the primary goal of psychotherapy (Brown, 1991). The therapist must be willing to let her make her own decision about whether to leave or stay with the batterer. If she decides to leave, therapist and client must be apprised of the fact that this period is probably the most dangerous for the battered woman. Indeed, many batterers become desperate when they are threatened with abandonment and are at their most dangerous then.

Statement 34:   ***When a woman leaves an abusive relationship, the likelihood of serious injury increases.***

This is TRUE. Studies show an increase in violence when the woman attempts to leave her husband (Giles-Sims, 1983). Both threats and actual attacks increase in number and the danger of a lethal outcome is highest when the woman tries to leave (Browne, 1987).

Statement 24:   ***Once a battered woman, always a battered woman.***

Statement 25:   ***Once a batterer, always a batterer.***

The first statement is FALSE, the second TRUE under most circumstances. Most battered women who leave a battering relationship go on to establish good relationships. Thus, battered women will not necessarily repeatedly pick men who batter. At the same time, men who batter, unless they are treated for partner abuse, are likely to go on to additional battering relationships (U.S. Commission on Civil Rights, 1982). Batterers who are not treated are likely to simply cycle women: As one refuses to put up with the abuse, he simply finds another whom he can control, at least for some time. This is because battering is not the result of a dysfunctional relationship, but rather the result of an individual man's dysfunctional relational style (Hansen & Harway, 1993).

Statement 28:   ***The diagnostic clue "accident prone" may appear in the history of some women.***

This statement is TRUE. Battered women are reluctant to reveal their abuse, because they have been made to feel responsible for it by society and persons from whom they might have previously sought help. However, women who have been battered repeatedly over time may have a history of many "accidents" in which they broke bones, sprained backs, tore ligaments, or had extensive contusions (Warshaw, 1989). This type of history should always be investigated for evidence of battering.

Statement 35:   ***The majority of battered women have been hit 1 to 3 times by their partner before being successfully helped.***

This statement is FALSE. The majority of battered women secretly endure abuse for years and may never receive help (Okun, 1986).

Statement 38: ***Upon hearing that a woman is in an abusive relationship, the majority of mental health professionals are most concerned about the woman's safety.***

Unfortunately this statement is FALSE. Mental health professionals should be most concerned about the woman's safety upon assessing that she is being battered. However, two studies (Hansen et al., 1991; Harway & Hansen, 1990) suggest otherwise. Most mental health professionals do not focus first on the woman's safety but rather are more concerned with issues such as the couple's interpersonal dynamics. Clearly more training is needed to ensure that battered women are adequately treated. As Goodstein and Page's research (1981) indicates, if the battering is not identified and dealt with immediately, it is unlikely that the woman will return for a second session.

Statement 44: ***Most women would rather experience psychological abuse than physical abuse.***

This statement is FALSE. Many women experience the psychological component of abuse as far more devastating than the physical component. In a review of the research by O'Leary (1999), ridicule is identified as the worst type of abuse.

COUPLE'S THERAPY

Statement 42: ***Couples who experience domestic violence and who seek counseling will usually tell their counselor about the violence.***

Statement 43: ***Working on relationship issues in couple's therapy will help increase the violence.***

Statement 42 is FALSE. O'Leary, Vivian, and Malone (1992) report that fewer than 5% of couples seeking marital therapy spontaneously report violence as a problem during the intake, yet as many as two-thirds of these couples admit to some form of violence on self-report measures. Other research supports the notion that couples experiencing spousal abuse very seldom tell their counselors about the violence (Holtzworth-Munroe et al., 1992). Ehrensaft and Vivian (1996) indicate that this is because couples do not consider the violence the problem; the violence is seen as infrequent and unstable and as secondary to other problems. Therefore, the clinician must always do an intake that will uncover spousal abuse if it exists.

Statement 43 is TRUE. Although there is some controversy about the use of couple's therapy with couples experiencing violence in the home, the consensus is that it is at best ineffective to do couple's therapy when violence exists, and at worst downright dangerous. In fact, couple's therapy may increase the risk of harm to the woman. Couple's therapy forces the couple to deal with problems in the relationship, which in turn is likely to lead to more conflict and perhaps increases in the violence. Moreover, couple's therapy is ineffective in stopping the violence because (as research by Jacobson et al. [1994] has demonstrated) the batterer's behaviors are independent of the behaviors of the victim.

LEGAL AND ETHICAL ISSUES

Statement 10: **If spouse abuse is suspected, mental health professionals are required by law to report it to the authorities.**

This statement is FALSE. Currently, there are no domestic violence mandated reporting laws for mental health practitioners in the United States unless the abused individual is a minor, an elder (over 65), or a dependent adult. In these cases, mental health professionals are mandated to report the violence (to the Department of Children's Services or the Department of Social Services in California; to other departments in other jurisdictions; Cervantes, 1993).

Statement 18: **In most parts of the country, police have been unsuccessful in protecting a battered woman.**

This statement is TRUE. A woman who has been battered may go to court to obtain a restraining order against her abuser. In some jurisdictions, this makes it easier for the police to arrest a batterer who is in violation of the order (Hart, 1993). However, the restraining order is only a piece of paper, and a batterer who is determined to harm his partner can do so. The police can only help when they are on the premises. In fact, police indicate that domestic violence calls are dangerous to them as well as to the woman.

Statement 39: ***The majority of abused senior citizens are beaten by their partners.***

TRUE. A number of articles suggest that many elder abuse victims are abused by their spouses and that some have suffered from years of chronic abuse (Pillemer & Suitor, 1991; Ramsey-Klawsnik, 1993). Although spouse abuse is not reportable in most jurisdictions, spouse abuse when the spouse is over 65 is reportable under elder abuse reporting statutes.

3

~/\/\

Assessment of
Spouse Abuse

How does a clinician know that the individual or couple presenting for therapy with a variety of presenting problems actually is experiencing spouse abuse? Spouse abuse is both difficult and very easy to assess. It can be relatively easy to assess for spouse abuse if you know the psychological characteristics that abused women present (men are sometimes the abused one, but quite rarely). Likewise, violent couples also come to therapy with telltale signs that an abuse-sensitized therapist can easily identify. Identifying abuse may be difficult for other therapists for other reasons. First, the client is unlikely to specifically address the violence as a presenting issue. Most abused women may be experiencing substantial denial. These women will resist the abuse label even after you have applied it to her circumstances. It is rare that the woman will present information about violence to you at intake, even if you ask her directly. However, if violence is not addressed, many clients will not return for a second visit (Goodstein & Page, 1981).

Second, the abused woman may initially be afraid to describe what she recognizes as violence, particularly in the presence of her husband. Third, abused women may be embarrassed and believe that you will think less of them for staying in the abusive relationship.

In this section, we will discuss how to assess for the existence of spouse abuse. We will separately discuss how to make this assessment when the woman presents as the client, when the man presents separately, when the couple or family come in for treatment, and when the children are brought in.

ASSESSING THE
WOMAN FOR SPOUSE ABUSE

DOES VIOLENCE EXIST?

> Mary Ann, a 38-year-old accountant, has sought therapy for depression. She describes her behavior as lethargic and unmotivated, having some difficulty sleeping at night, and easily teary. Mary Ann is married with three children, and stably employed for the last 10 years. Her husband, Jim, 42, an engineer, is said to be a good provider, a good father, and a loyal mate.

Even though you are not aware of it at the time, Mary Ann is a typical battered woman. A battered woman is likely to present for therapy complaining about everything else, but never mentioning that she is in a violent relationship. How then does the therapist know to assess for violence and evaluate the specific needs of the client? Some excerpts from Mary Ann's intake interview demonstrate a possible approach.

Therapist: Tell me some more about your tiredness and trouble sleeping. How long have these problems been going on?

Mary Ann: For some time now. But recently they have gotten worse. And it's starting to affect my ability to do my job.

Therapist: Why now? Has something happened recently that has been bothering you?

Mary Ann: Nothing really new. I do worry about my children.

Therapist: Oh? Why is that?

Mary Ann: (whispers) I'm afraid about what they see or hear.

Therapist: Is there something specific?

Mary Ann: (quietly) Not really.

Therapist: Tell me about your relationship with Jim.

Mary Ann: Jim is a good father and a good provider. He doesn't drink or smoke. He's in good physical shape. As far as I know he's always been faithful to me.

Therapist: How would you describe your marriage?

Mary Ann: Okay. No different from others, I guess.

Therapist: All relationships are special. What's special about yours?

Mary Ann: It's really pretty average. But I guess others seem to have more fun. We're always arguing.

Therapist: Is that why you're not sleeping?

Mary Ann: Well, I keep thinking about it. . . .

Therapist: Tell me about your most recent argument.

Mary Ann: I wanted to buy a new couch for the family room and Jim told me that we couldn't afford it. Now we both bring in pretty good salaries and I know we have $8,000 in a savings account. So, I couldn't understand why Jim would say we can't afford it. We have had the same couch now for 12 years and the entire right side is ripped. It's embarrassing.

Therapist: So, what happened?

Mary Ann: We kept arguing and (she begins to cry). . . .

Therapist: (hands tissue) and then. . . .

Mary Ann: I'm so tired of struggling, for everything. Even a measly couch!

Therapist: And. . . .

Mary Ann: (barely audibly) He called me a bitch and told me that no wonder I have no friends. That nobody could ever stand me. Then he pushed the coffee table over and he broke my best Wedgewood candy holder. Then he slapped me.

Therapist: That seems like quite a strong reaction! He struck you. . . .

Mary Ann: Yes . . . but not too hard.

Therapist: He struck you harder before?

Mary Ann: Well, yes. . . .

The intake interview may not always provide evidence that violence is present in the client's relationship, as readily as presented here. All intake interviews should include questions about conflict and violence in the relationship, even where there is otherwise no evidence of violence (just as most therapists routinely ask about alcohol and drug abuse). A direct question such as "Has your husband (partner) ever hit you?" may not yield relevant information. She may answer "No," partly because of her shame in being the recipient of physical abuse, but also because she may have been pushed, had objects thrown at her, or had weapons pointed at her and thus technically may not have been "hit" by her husband. Instead, a series of questions directed at the couple's style of conflict resolution may be more effective. That is why our therapist asked about the couple's most recent disagreement. The therapist might also have asked: "How do you and your husband deal with disagreements?" Alternately she might have asked: "When your husband is extremely upset with you, what does he say and do?" or "In any of these disagreements, has your husband ever touched you physically?" (to be followed by inquiries about pushing, physically holding her down, or whether he has used his body or any type of instrument to strike or physically hurt her). The therapist might instead have asked: "Has your husband ever been abusive with you, either verbally or physically?"

There are a number of different ways of putting forth these or similar questions. First, it is important to be sensitive to the characteristics of shame, guilt, embarrassment, and fear that may prevent the woman from responding to direct questioning. Sensitivity and persistence are essential. Second, it is important to recognize that a single question may not yield very reliable information about the presence or absence of violence and of the possible danger to the woman. Third, it is important to persevere and ask follow-up questions even though the woman denies any violence in her relationship. As the self-quiz earlier pointed out (see Chapter 2), women who ended up in hospital emergency rooms after being battered had previously seen a therapist, but only for one session and the therapist *never asked about the violence*. An alert therapist will err on the side of thoroughness when inquiring about spousal abuse. We suggest that you use the "freeze frame approach." Similar to a piece of film that can be advanced one frame at a time (and when necessary, can be paused – or frozen – on an individual frame), this process allows detailed examination of a possibly abusive interaction between your client and her partner. It allows for the slowing down and detailing of the memory of what was surely an emotional interaction for your client. The battered woman's tendency to minimize or deny what she has experienced may cause her to jump from precipitating event to conclusion without describing the abuse that may have occurred between those two points in time. For example, revisiting the interaction with Mary Ann (or with a client who was less forthcoming with the information), the interchange might have gone like this:

Therapist: Tell me about your most recent argument.
Mary Ann: I wanted to buy a new couch for the family room and Jim told me that we couldn't afford it. Now we both bring in pretty good salaries and I know we have $8,000 in a savings account. So, I couldn't understand why Jim would say we can't afford it. We have had the same couch now for 12 years and the entire right side is ripped. It's embarrassing.
Therapist: So, what happened?
Mary Ann: We kept arguing for a while, and well, I am not buying a new couch.

Mary Ann, in her description of the argument with her husband, has skipped over virtually all of the details of the fight. Without this information, a therapist who has no background information about Mary Ann and her family would likely not realize that the interaction in question included physical violence.

The freeze frame approach, by slowing down the presentation of information, encourages the client to describe the interaction without skipping over the violent details. It also gives the therapist substantial information about a typical interaction between her client and the husband. Another way to encourage the client to give the necessary detail is to indicate wanting to be a "fly on the wall, observing the process of the interaction."

Looking again at Mary Ann's description of her argument with her husband, encouraging her to provide more detail through the freeze frame approach might look something like this:

Therapist: Tell me about your most recent argument.

Mary Ann: I wanted to buy a new couch for the family room and Jim told me that we couldn't afford it. Now we both bring in pretty good salaries and I know we have $8,000 in a savings account. So, I couldn't understand why Jim would say we can't afford it. We have had the same couch now for 12 years and the entire right side is ripped. It's embarrassing.

Therapist: So, what happened?

Mary Ann: We kept arguing for a while, and well, I am not buying a new couch.

Therapist: Wait, hold on a second. Let's go back to the beginning of the argument. You wanted to buy a new couch for the family room. So what did you say to Jim?

Mary Ann: I told him how embarrassed I was about the couch and that I wanted to buy a new one.

Therapist: So, what did Jim say?

Mary Ann: He told me that we didn't need a new couch and that I was also spending too much money.

Therapist: So what did you say to that?

Mary Ann: I told him that the only money I spent was on groceries or things the children needed for school.

Therapist: So then what happened?

Mary Ann: He called me a bad name.

Therapist: What was that?

Mary Ann: He called me a bitch.

Therapist: And then what happened?

Mary Ann: I began to cry.

Therapist: So how did Jim respond to that?
Mary Ann: He slapped me.
Therapist: Where did he slap you? How hard?

By asking for minute details about the interaction, this therapist is getting a good picture of how the argument proceeded and how it moved from the use of civil words, to insults, to physical violence. It provides the therapist with the information needed to assess for the existence of spousal abuse.

Some abused women may still complete the intake interview convincing you that they have not experienced violence (although the likelihood of this is much reduced through the above-described approach). Abused women have acquired characteristics that serve both to protect them and keep them in their abusive relationships. Follingstad et al. (1988) describe the variety of coping styles that battered women might adopt in coming to terms with the abuse. These coping styles allow the woman to survive the battering, but serve to ensure that she remains in the abusive relationship. One style of coping involves the woman's conceptualization of why the abuse has occurred. Among the conceptualizations acquired by battered women to understand the battering are (a) denial of the seriousness of the injury she has experienced, (b) attribution of the blame for the violence to forces outside the control of both partners, (c) blaming herself for the violence, (d) denial of her emotional or practical options, (e) wanting to save her partner by helping him overcome his problem while continuing to tolerate the abuse, and (f) her commitment to enduring the violence for the sake of some higher commitment such as religion or tradition (Ferraro & Johnson, 1983). The battered woman's denial in the face of your persistent inquiry may be a clear signal that she is not yet ready to address the characteristics of the abusive relationship. However, you are ethically bound to provide appropriate treatment, because your client may also be in physical danger. Therefore, it is important for you to know that your client is being abused.

When persistent inquiry fails to inform you of violence in a relationship, alternate approaches are available. Battered women often share a number of presenting characteristics with other survivors of trauma. Globally, these characteristics have been described as those of Posttraumatic Stress Disorder (PTSD). These symptoms may include depression (which might be the result of a common coping mechanism of battered women: Expressing anger toward the batterer could well have the effect of increasing the violence. In contrast, repressing the intense anger experienced in response to a beating may instead have greater survival value);

reexperiencing the trauma through nightmares, flashbacks, and/or intrusive thoughts of the trauma; numbing to the external world and a variety of anxiety-related symptoms such as sleep disturbance, eating disorders, or substance abuse; and avoidance of stimuli associated with the trauma and an intensification of anxiety when confronted with reminders of the trauma. Other presenting characteristics may be a diminished decision-making and problem-solving style (attributed by researchers to repeated exposure to the trauma), suicidality, somatization, hypervigilance, emotional lability, and victimization of others (see Table 1 below).

Psychotherapists working with battered women may be surprised to see the woman blaming herself for causing the abuse. They may also notice that she blames herself for not being able to modify the occurrence of the abuse or for tolerating the abuse. However, this coping style is described by Miller and Porter (1983) as allowing the woman to maintain the illusion that she is still in control of her life. She is therefore allowed to believe that a "just world" exists where people get what they deserve and bad things do not happen to good people. Unfortunately her perception of control and a just world often serve to keep her in the abusive situation and frustrates the efforts of those who would encourage her to leave. In support of this position, Hendricks-Matthews (1982) reports that therapy is less successful for women who self-blame than for those who blame their batterers.

After the initial battering incident, the woman often sees the violence as an aberration and as something that she may be able to control. She then focuses on identifying ways of preventing the abuse from recurring. Eventually, she may become discouraged. Some research suggests that battered women have a significantly higher external locus of control than a normative sample, or a belief that she has little impact on her fate. Battered women who are in longer relationships appear to have a higher

---

TABLE 1:

**Common PTSD Symptoms
Found Among Battered Women**

Depression	Suicidality
Anxiety	Intrusive Thoughts
Sleep Disorders	Somatization
Eating Disorders	Victimization of Others
Substance Abuse	Hypervigilance

external locus of control than battered women in shorter relationships (Cheney & Bleker, 1982). Similarly, Feldman (1983) found that battered women who continued in their relationships had a more external locus of control than did either battered women who left the relationship or women not in battering relationships. This research suggests that there may be characteristics about being in or continuing in abusive relationships that erode a woman's sense of control over her own destiny and ultimately result in the passivity or numbness that some have reported in battered women (see Hanks & Rosenbaum [1977], or Walker's [1984] explanations of the battered woman syndrome and learned helplessness).

You may choose to use an abuse inventory (e.g., the Abuse Risk Inventory for Women [Yegidis, 1989]; Hudson & McIntosh's [1981] Index of Spouse Abuse; Bodin's [1992] Relationship Conflict Inventory) or some other screening test to ensure that all presenting symptoms of spouse abuse are recognized. Because many abused women experience symptoms related to Posttraumatic Stress Disorder, you might consider using an instrument such as the Trauma Symptom Checklist (Briere & Runtz, 1989).

Your first task as a clinician, then, is to identify the violence experienced by a client who may not be forthcoming with the information about her abuse. You would be wise to keep in mind the possibility of domestic violence with all clients who present with some or all of the constellation of presenting characteristics listed previously.

An area that requires special attention is the impact of psychological abuse. Psychological abuse has been identified as including rejection, humiliation, exploitation, and use of male privilege and degradation (Follingstad & DeHart, 2000). Also included are ridicule, jealousy, restriction, threats to change marital status, damage to property, and threats of abuse (O'Leary, 1999). Women who experience psychological abuse may not respond to questions of marital aggression and may in fact see themselves as experiencing the expected conflict that occurs in many marriages. Such characteristics have significant impact on self-perception and on the woman's perception of her own contribution to the marital discord. Psychologists are known to disagree on what constitutes emotional/psychological abuse, suggesting that these components are even more likely to be overlooked or identified as abuse (Follingstad & DeHart, 2000).

HOW DANGEROUS IS THE VIOLENCE?

As discussed before, the therapist's first task is to identify whether violence is a factor for the client. The therapist's next task is to ascertain the level of danger that the client faces. Epidemiological research of domestic violence clearly indicates that conjugal assaults tend to have more serious consequences than other types of assault (see Harway & Hansen, 1993a, for more detailed statistics). Many women endure repeated batterings, often of increasing severity, within a relatively short time frame (e.g., in one study [Okun, 1986], women experienced more than five assaults every 4 weeks, with 20% being battered twice or more per week). The injuries that battered women report range from lacerations and fractures to bullet and stab wounds. In many cases, domestic violence is extreme enough to result in murder; lethality in cases of wife battering is most likely to occur when the woman tries to leave (Browne, 1987).

These statistics make it imperative for you to assess the danger to the client early in treatment. Questions about the existence of weapons within the home must be asked. Likewise, you should obtain a detailed battering history about the use or threat of use of weapons, including common household weapons such as carving knives and the like. The progression of the abuse should also be documented. Seldom does domestic violence begin in the most severe form. Usually there is a pattern of increasingly severe emotional abuse which may include insults, name-calling, demeaning comments, threats, and accusations, or intense questioning about normal daily activities. Isolation and intimidation may be used. The man may have used his physical presence or size or threatened her with violence (e.g., standing in the doorway so that she is unable to leave; taking her car keys, money, checkbook, or credit cards so that she cannot leave; unplugging the phone so she cannot call police, friends, or family). At some point, the emotional and verbal abuse may have graduated to the use of physical objects as threats (e.g., throwing objects, breaking personal items, tearing clothes, or driving recklessly to scare her). The physical violence may begin with pushing and shoving which then can lead to slapping, biting, choking, hair pulling, kicking, backhanding, punching, and eventually to the use of weapons. Not every batterer will necessarily follow the same pattern, nor will each situation of abuse graduate to the same behaviors. However, you need to be aware of the possibilities of such incremental changes in the violence.

Assessing the extent of danger the client is in must be ongoing. You have a responsibility to be aware of the potential danger to the client at each step in the therapy and to teach her how to protect herself.

HOW SEVERELY AFFECTED IS THE CLIENT?

The third and final level of assessment that must be considered in the treatment of the battered woman concerns the impact of the abuse on the client. The TRIADS model developed by Burgess, Hartman, and Kelly (1990) may be useful to consider. TRIADS is a trauma assessment tool of more general utility than assessing for battering. Useful for all types of trauma, it gives clinicians a quick sense of the extent of emotional injury experienced by the battered woman.

TRIADS is an acronym for *T*ypes of abuse (physical, sexual, psychological), *R*ole relationships between victim and offender (intrafamilial vs. extrafamilial), *I*ntensity (number of acts and offenders), *A*ffective state (expressed vs. controlled demeanor), *D*uration (length of time), and *S*tyle of abuse (single, patterned, or ritualistic). To the extent that a woman has been abused both physically and psychologically as well as forced to engage in sex acts against her will by a spouse or life partner repeatedly (especially after a prior history of abuse) and over a long period of time, she is likely to be most damaged. Her affective state will also indicate the extent of damage, in that a client who is overly controlled is likely to be more affected than a client who is emotionally labile. Not every woman will experience Posttraumatic Stress Disorder, but it is important to assess this early so that proper treatment can be implemented.

The assessment of impact of abuse on a woman's functioning should be made whether she is currently in the abusive relationship or recently removed from it, as she is likely to have symptoms for some time after leaving the abusive relationship.

ASSESSING THE
BATTERER FOR SPOUSE ABUSE

The batterer rarely presents in therapy of his own volition. He is much more likely to seek therapy only when court referred subsequent to a violent episode or when referred by his wife as the result of an ultimatum prior to divorce. Because of the referral modality, it will usually be clear when a batterer presents for therapy.

How then should you identify a male client who enters therapy for some reason other than battering? The research on batterer characteristics and typologies concludes that for the most part there is no clear batterer profile, although there may be several subtypes of batterers (Gondolf, 1993; Holtzworth-Munroe & Stuart, 1994). Identifying batterers based on symptomatology or characteristics may be difficult. Gondolf recommends assessing how the client reacts to control and anger cues. O'Neil and Egan (1993) suggest that the clinician assess whether the male client' is in gender-role conflict. This manifests as rigid, sexist, or restrictive gender-role socialization which may present as restrictive emotionality and with a focus on power and competition issues. In particular, key is the assessment of the man's perception of power conflicts as internal, caused by others, or expressed by others. O'Neil and Nadeau (1999) hypothesize that "gender-role socialization, distorted gender-role schemas, gender-role conflicts, defense mechanisms and self protective defense strategies are primary factors that predispose men to be violent against women" (p. 89).

Some of the signs we have learned to look for include (these are especially important to look for when doing an intake with a couple):

- Reported fear on the part of the partner. This seems to be the single best indicator that some form of abuse is present in the relationship.
- Use of win/lose strategies in resolving conflicts. Because this is a common mind-set of batterers, the use of such strategies serve as a red flag. This is especially so when he appears willing to "hurt" his partner in order to win. When he deems it necessary to emotionally overpower or control his partner in resolving conflict, this is almost always related to abuse.
- A pattern of controlling or attempting to control his partner in minor as well as more important interactions. When the clinician feels controlled by the client in the session, this too may be a red flag.
- Isolation of the partner.
- Blaming of all negative outcomes on the partner; portraying the partner as crazy or stupid and justifying his own negative behavior on that basis. By contrast, victims usually blame themselves even when they are not at fault.
- Lack of empathy for the partner.
- Evidence of self-righteousness or knowing THE right way or answer.
- Willingness to admit to specific behaviors but not others. For example, batterers will almost never admit to being violent or abusive. However, they are more willing to admit to specific behaviors, for example, having slapped or pushed their partner. This is partly because batterers tend to minimize the violence they perpetrate.

- • Reports of repeated injuries to the victim (e.g., walking into doors, slipping and falling, etc.).
- • Excessive jealousy often based on little supporting evidence; a sense of being obsessed with the partner.

Tom, 48, is a successful physician. He has been married for 10 years to Ellen, 39, who prior to their marriage was employed as an operating room nurse. This is Tom's second marriage, Ellen's first. They have no children of their own, although Tom has grown twin boys from a prior marriage. Tom has entered therapy because he is worried that Ellen may be having an affair and his best friend has recommended therapy as the way to get some ideas about how to handle the situation. A first interview with Tom indicates that Tom is convinced that he has been an excellent husband and that Ellen's lack of responsiveness to his sexual advances is because she is involved with someone else. He describes her as having become increasingly distant to him and can identify nothing in his own behavior or their relationship which can account for the changes. He also indicates that Ellen has been more reluctant of late to keep up with her household responsibilities and with the help she has always provided to him in his medical office. During the intake interview, Tom repeatedly blames her for the changes which have taken place and states, "If she would only have listened to me and not taken the course at the university, none of this would have happened. She has responsibilities and she is not living up to these as we had agreed."

Spousal abuse may have roots in gender-roles, because men's gender-role socialization teaches them that being masculine means maintaining power over women. They may use power over their life partners in destructive and often violent ways, to the extent that their masculine identity is dependent on this belief system. Thus, identifying a man's belief about gender-roles is likely to provide important clues as to his likelihood to embark on psychologically or physically abusive paths. O'Neil and Nadeau (1999) report that men learn sexist values and stereotypes that influence how they relate to women (as well as others). The Masculine Mystique, a set of sexist values and beliefs, defines how optimal masculinity looks. Negative emotions such as anger, fear, guilt, anxiety, shame, self-hatred, hurt, loss, and sadness are responded to by eliciting fears of femininity and fears of being emasculated that threaten men's masculine gender identity. In turn, these fears are temporarily neutralized by powerful self-protective strategies which include power and control, and restrictive emotionality which often lead to physical violence when in the presence of triggering events. Because these self-protective mechanisms are temporary, however, they do not effectively resolve the conflict and emotions over the long term and set up cyclical patterns. Results of a recent study of how abusive men react to stress (Williams, Umberson, & Anderson, 2002) indicate that these men do not show signs of depression or other typical reactions to stress, but instead that the feelings of stress build up and are released as bursts of violence.

Evans' (Segel-Evans, 1994; and in Harway & Evans, 1996) "Cycle of Feeling Avoidance" describes how this process may operate and provides important clinical clues to treating batterers. In describing the cycle of violence first popularized by Lenore Walker (1979), Evans explains the dynamics of the tension build-up phase (see Table 2 below). He indicates that this phase is the result of feelings defended against; for example, the man may experience guilt or shame about something either in the present or the past, fear abandonment, or simply feel hurt. However, these feelings are not consciously experienced. His inability to experience his feelings leads in turn to one or more defenses against those feelings, for example, abuse of alcohol or drugs, the search for negative ex-

TABLE 2:

The Cycle of Feeling Avoidance

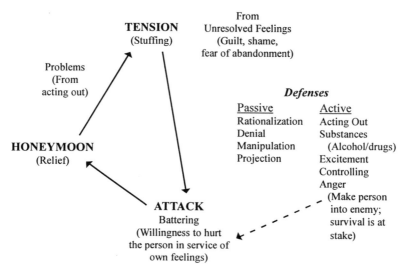

TENSION
(Stuffing)

From
Unresolved Feelings
(Guilt, shame,
fear of abandonment)

Problems
(From
acting out)

Defenses

Passive	Active
Rationalization	Acting Out
Denial	Substances
Manipulation	(Alcohol/drugs)
Projection	Excitement
	Controlling
	Anger
	(Make person
	into enemy;
	survival is at
	stake)

HONEYMOON
(Relief)

ATTACK
Battering
(Willingness to hurt
the person in service of
own feelings)

citement, or blaming his spouse. The use of alcohol or drugs may defuse the underlying unrecognized feelings. Similarly, blaming the spouse – who is quickly seen as the enemy – leads to attacking that enemy (Walker's explosion phase) which in turn releases the built-up tension. This explosion is then followed by what Walker describes as the honeymoon period (which Evans notes may get shorter and shorter over time). Inevitably, because life brings with it many problems, and in fact the violent episode has created additional stresses in this relationship, tension will build up again and the cycle will continue to repeat itself. This is largely because of the batterer's inability to recognize his feelings and to take responsibility for them. Thus, another diagnostic sign that you may look for is a man's inability to recognize his feelings and his externalization of the blame for the things that happen to him. These characteristics will not in all cases signify a violent man. However, they are important styles to attend to. Evans describes the cycle as one where the man attempts to control and where, regardless of what the other party does, the cycle continues. He also indicates that an abuser may be violent only in his intimate relationships, but he will also be controlling and abusive in most of his relationships. Thus, you may well find it useful to identify how a man who is suspected of being violent behaves in other more distant relationships, including how the abuser responds to the therapist.

ASSESSING A
COUPLE FOR VIOLENCE

When a couple presents for marital counseling, the clinician is faced with the most difficult task of all in terms of assessing for the presence and severity of violence. A study by Holtzworth-Munroe et al. (1992) indicates that a history of marital violence is present in far more maritally distressed couples than are otherwise identified. Thus, the therapist who sees a couple for otherwise run-of-the-mill marital problems must always assess for spousal abuse. This assessment is complicated by the fact that a battered woman, even one not in denial, would be unlikely (even unwise) to reveal the violence in the presence of her batterer. She may fear (often legitimately) that she would suffer the consequences after the session. For this reason, you should always conduct intake interviews with couples in such a way that at least some portion of the intake is spent alone with each partner (even where there is no mention of abuse during the initial telephone contact). It is helpful to let the couple know at first phone contact that the intake interview will be composed of four segments. The first segment will be a time when the couple together will provide a brief overview of the presenting issues (and where the clinician will look for such telltale signs as described on pp. 43-44). This segment will of necessity be relatively short. A second segment will be an interview with the female partner alone (this is based on the odds that if there is abuse, she is the likely victim). This order is predicated on the fact that the battered woman is more likely to provide an accurate account of the conflict, including revealing her abuse (or to specify the severity of abuse if the couple presents because of the violence) if she is alone in the room with you. Being seen first makes it easier for you to begin your intake with the male partner armed with information about the abuse, if any exists. The information about the relationship is elicited using the same types of questions described in the section relating to assessment of the single woman client (in particular the freeze frame method described earlier). If battering is reported in this individual interview by the woman, the dilemma of the therapist becomes what to do with the information (and to provide her with enough safety measures in the short period of your time together). Once your brief intake of the woman is complete, you should have a reasonable sense of whether there is violence in this relationship. Armed with this information, the intake with the male partner will be somewhat easier. Batterers can be extremely charming, are also likely to minimize any violence in which they might participate, and are usually extremely resistant to acknowledging having used any form of physical violence. Even when you use the freeze frame method to ascertain how interactions proceed between the man and his partner, it may be difficult to elicit a description of violence from a batterer. The need to control the therapeutic session and the charming nature of most batterers may make it extremely difficult for you to properly identify the existence of the violence. However, if in phase two of the intake you have found evidence of violence, this information will serve you well in getting the batterer to acknowledge violent behavior. At the very least, it will allow you to bulldoggedly pursue an admission of abuse from the batterer. Such an admission is important because, in phase four of the intake, you will bring the couple back together to discuss treatment recommendations. It will be important that the recommendations for treatment for the batterer seem to be based on information he (rather than his partner) has provided you. As we will describe later, the initial treatment of choice with a violent couple is not to work in a couple's modality. Rather, the ideal treatment for a batterer is a batterer treatment group. Initial goals of the batterer's treatment will be to help him recognize and openly acknowledge his violence. Until he does so, the information gained from the woman (individually at intake) must continue to be protected. Of course, only then can the real treatment of the battering behavior begin. Meanwhile, the battered woman can be provided supportive treatment in individual therapy and at some later point encouraged to seek a battered women's group.

Presentation of the treatment recommendations must be delicately handled. In order to ensure the continued well-being of the woman, you cannot overtly implement a treatment plan that focuses on the violence or refers to the violence (to do so would endanger the woman and make her vulnerable to a battering after the session). You may want to use language such as: "George, in our time together, you told me that you became very angry with Susan during a recent argument. As a result, you did some things about which you are not very proud. Susan, you acknowledged some individual issues that you need to focus on as well. My recommendations are that the first part of treatment be reserved to working on your individual issues and once these have been appropriately resolved, then we should schedule some time together to work on the issues that the two of you have as a couple. George, I would like to refer you to a group that a colleague of mine runs. Participants are all men who have issues with their partners that are very similar to yours and I think you will greatly benefit from being with them for a few months." Recommendations to his partner would be to seek out individual therapy with a therapist other than yourself. This is to avoid any sense he might have that you are aligning with his partner if you were to treat her. Also, if the couple does decide to pursue couple's therapy down the line, you will be available to do the couple's work without any perceived alignment with one member of the couple. You cannot recommend that the woman enter a battered women's group because doing so would immediately cause him to bristle. This recommendation is better left to her individual therapist who may recommend she seek out such a group once she is in individual treatment.

Couple's therapy is not generally believed to be an effective modality when violence occurs in the relationship. This issue is still equivocal among some practitioners, but many localities require single-sex batterers' group treatment for court-mandated perpetrators because of evidence from both clinical and empirical venues about the dangers of couple's therapy. This is discussed in more detail in Chapter 4.

ASSESSING CHILDREN FOR THE
EFFECTS OF SPOUSAL ABUSE

Our knowledge and understanding of the impact of spouse abuse on children has increased greatly in the decade since the publication of the previous edition of this volume. At that time, we knew that witnessing spouse abuse had a negative impact on children and that children might express this impact through internalizing or externalizing behavior at a greater rate than children who had not witnessed spouse abuse. Currently we are recognizing that the actual number of children who witness such abuse is likely to far exceed the actual number of spouse abuse victims themselves (multiple-child families). Since the publication of our last volume, considerable effort has gone into exploring the impact on these additional victims, the children. Our increased understanding can be effectively organized into three areas: the exploration of the factors that contribute to the emotional and behavioral impact of abuse on children, the nature of the impact on children's development and functioning, and the emotional disturbances that are likely to result from these experiences. Assessing the child who witnesses abuse requires that all these aforementioned concerns be addressed.

EXPLORATION OF FACTORS

First and foremost, therapists need to be aware that children and their parents perceive spouse abuse differently as it occurs. Reports of what the child saw and the child is aware of, what the parent thought the child saw and is aware of, and what the parent perceives actually happened all are important components of any evaluation (Levendosky, Huth-Bocks, & Semel, 2002). *What the child saw* is likely to have the greatest impact on the child's emotional response and subsequent emotional development. Did the child see one parent strike the other parent? Did the child see one parent pick up a knife and threaten the other parent? Actual observation of abuse is shown to have a major impact on the child's emotional functioning (Jouriles et al., 1996). Likewise, *what the child knows to be happening in the family* is also important. The child hearing a parent striking the other parent and hearing the battering occurring, hearing the threats that precede the sounds, witnessing the trips to the emergency room, leaving the house and going to the shelter, all increase children's knowledge of the occurrence of abuse whether or not they actually saw all the events (O'Brien et al., 1994). Knowledge rather than actual observation can have a different impact on the child and needs to be assessed as well. Research suggests what the child has observed and what the child is aware of are likely the greatest indicators of the emotional impact on the child (O'Brien et al., 1994). However, *the parent's perception of what the child knows and has seen* is also important (O'Hearn, Margolin, & John, 1997). Is there convergence between their viewpoints? How much the parent knows of the child's perception will be an important factor in the subsequent therapeutic intervention both with the parent and with the family members. Children tend to know more about the abuse in the family than the parents think they know (Rosenberg, 1987). However, *the victimized parent's report of what actually happened* is also important. Again the actual violence, as well as the child's perception of violence, are both important factors in treatment (Grych, Seid, & Fincham, 1992). For clinicians, we recommend the use of informed therapeutic interviews rather than structured assessment tools that are more likely to be designed for research purposes. Informed therapeutic interviews from a knowledgeable and skilled clinician are likely to yield a more individualized and sensitive clinical approach to future treatment.

Many other factors contribute to the experiences of children who witness abuse and should be included in an assessment (Graham-Bermann, 1998). The *frequency* of the violence is an important factor. Is the violence a single episode in a couple that regularly resolves conflict successfully or is it a day-to-day occurrence? The child's perception could range from a belief that the violence was an accident, with a single occurrence, to a chronic fear and anxiety when violence is an everyday occurrence. Also, the chronicity of the violence could have an impact: Did the episode of violence occur over a few months during a time of extreme family stress, or is this the only response to conflict the child has ever known? The *severity* of the violence is another factor that must be assessed (Graham-Bermann, 1998). Is the violence life threatening? Is it a shove or a slap; does it result in trips to the emergency room; does it leave marks, cuts, or bruises? Also are *weapons involved?* The use of knives and guns in the couple's altercations are shown to have significantly greater impact on the child's functioning, particularly if the child actually observed the use of the weapons (Jouriles et al., 1998). What *type of violence* has the child seen? Is it the type of violence that the child might also engage in with siblings and peers, or is it more adult violence such as choking or sexual violence? All violence is important to address, and children's individual responses differ. Witnessing psychological abuse without physical abuse is known to have a long-term impact on the child's development (Fantuzzo et al., 1991). All these factors are important in any evaluation of the child.

Requiring careful attention is the assessment of child abuse that occurs concurrently with the spouse abuse. An estimated 30% to 70% of all children who witness spouse abuse are victims themselves. For this reason, in cases of spouse abuse, not only will the child's response to the adult violence need to be assessed but also a very thorough assessment of possible child abuse should be conducted immediately. When the children are themselves victims of abuse as well as witnesses, the emotional impact on the children is significantly greater than either condition alone (Yexley, Borowsky, & Ireland, 2002). Children often become part of the couple's dynamic and may be included in the controlling behavior of the abusive partner; they are often used to manipulate control within the couple dyad (Levendosky & Graham-Bermann, 2000). In addition, witnessing a sibling being victimized as well as a parent is likely to increase the significance of the child's experience. Boys are more likely to be the target of the physical abuse, possibly as they are more likely to misbehave, be aggressive, or physically intervene to try to stop the violence.

Families who present with spouse abuse are often experiencing other contextual stressors that will have a serious impact on the functioning of their children. Researchers attempt to identify the separate and comparative contribution of each stressor. However, from a clinical perspective, identification of the specific stressors and assessment of severity, frequency, and chronicity for the specific family contributes more to successful therapeutic interventions than a debate about relative impact. Each child's response is likely to vary, and recognition of stressors will expand to include multiple areas for intervention. Such stressors include concurrent abuse of alcohol and drugs (McBurnett et al., 2001), poverty, and frequent incarceration of one or the other parent. If the family goes to a shelter to avoid the abuse or is in one during the time of the assessment, this can act as an additional stressor contributing to the sense of homelessness experienced by the child (Fantuzzo et al., 1991; Spaccarelli, Sandler, & Roosa, 1994). Many families experiencing child abuse frequently relocate and changing homes and schools adds additional stress to children (Spaccarelli et al., 1994). The importance of parents or caretakers as mediators for children's perception of stress is recognized under conditions of traumatic violence (Levendosky & Graham-Bermann, 1998). When the traumatic violence occurs between parents, the effectiveness of the parents' ability to mediate the intensity of the impact is diminished due to their need to defend themselves from the abuse that is directed at them personally. In addition, the effectiveness of the parent to mediate the intensity of the impact of other stressful factors such as poverty, substance abuse, and relocation is likely to be impaired as well.

Likewise, spouse abuse often includes increased isolation of family members from other sources of support. Therefore, the children are less likely to have the opportunity to benefit from the mediation from stress by other nurturing caretakers.

Other forms of spouse abuse, including psychological aggression, are important to consider when assessing the child. We are beginning to find that among children who have witnessed spouse abuse, other forms of abuse also have a major impact upon them (Levendosky & Graham-Bermann, 1998). Such abuse includes, but is not limited to, violence against objects, verbal threats, insults, and demeaning comments. During the assessment process, such forms of violence are as important as physical violence when examining the child's emotional and behavioral well-being. This perspective is true both for children living in their own home and coming to therapy and for children living in shelters. Children who have witnessed physical violence are likely to respond with great intensity to the threat of any aggression rather than to become desensitized to it (Levendosky & Graham-Bermann, 2000). Such factors are critical when approaching the treatment of the child; the mere absence of physical violence, or violence in the past, is not likely to alleviate the child's symptomatology, particularly if the other forms of abuse continue or contact with the abuser continues to occur.

IMPACT ON DEVELOPMENT

Children vary in how they perceive the violence and their perception of their own role in the occurrence. As children develop socially, cognitively, and emotionally, they vary in their perception of their own responsibility for actions that occur around them. In families where spouse abuse occurs, children vary in their perception of their own responsibility for the marital discord. Factors such as their perception of the threat to themselves can increase the aggressiveness of children, particularly boys (E. M. Cummings, Davies, & Simpson, 1994). The perception that they are to blame for the marital discord can increase the emotional impairment of girls in particular (E. M. Cummings et al., 1994). The actual destructiveness of the violence can increase children's perception of their responsibility for it. However, children's perception of their ability to effectively reduce the conflict can decrease the negative impact of the violence on their emotional and behavioral functioning and should be assessed as well. What coping strategies children employ and what options they perceive themselves to have are important components of an evaluation. Safety of the child is first and foremost, and the clinician needs to determine if the child's coping strategy is putting the child at greater risk. Risky behavior would include interceding with the parents to stop the violence, leaving the home in the middle of the night to get away, and other such solutions.

How children process the violence they observe is a function of many internal factors. Among them, children's perception of the family's emotional climate has an impact on the emotional impact of the violence (E. M. Cummings, 1998). Do children perceive the climate as threatening and unsafe, or are there sufficient sources of emotional nurturance and warmth? How do they interpret the violence they witness? Do they perceive it as justified, provoked, or life threatening? What are the coping strategies available to the children? Do their coping strategies remove them from harm's way and gain them access to emotional support, such as fleeing from the environment to another supportive adult, or do their coping strategies put children at risk, such as when attempting to be the peacekeeper and becoming instead the victim of the violent assault?

The children's temperament is important to consider when assessing the impact of witnessing spouse abuse. Children's temperament is known to consistently interact with the temperament of parents and other family members. Temperament is likely to be a discerning factor when assessing children's response to violence and also the responses that are elicited from the parents (E. M. Cummings, 1998). For example, children who are irritable, impulsive, and have a hard time remaining calm may get in the middle of the parental conflict; children who are quiet and reserved may become further withdrawn when witnessing violence.

Earlier research focused on the belief that children modeled violence and therefore children modeled the behavior of the aggressive parent (Graham-Bermann, 1998). Because modeling is often gender specific, boys who witnessed the aggressive behavior of violent fathers were perceived to be likely to grow to become aggressive spouses. Studies that have focused on the interpersonal relationships of sons, dating, and so forth, are inconclusive (Levendosky et al., 2002). More promising work suggests that children who witness psychological abuse may develop a controlling, demeaning, and humiliating approach to conflict resolution (Graham-Bermann, 1998). Much of the research since the last edition has focused on the social cognitive theories, theories that are consistent with this response to psychological abuse (Graham-Bermann, 1998).

An expansion of the previous perception of modeling continues to examine the impact from a social learning theory perspective, but in the form of learning complex behavior scripts. Either children learn to manipulate, cajole, and coerce others to get their needs met, or the converse learning takes place: submission, self-blame, and giving up in the face of difficulty (E. M. Cummings, 1998). Power and control tactics are learned as well as physical aggression, and children acquire an inadequate repertoire of social skills. Thus, conflict resolution skills are an area of major developmental gap among children who witness abuse (E. M. Cummings, 1998).

One of the most intriguing explanations of children's responses postulates that children who witness abuse learn distorted perceptions of relationships, especially family roles and gender roles. Rather than the violence having a direct impact on adjustment, the violence impacts and distorts the internalized relationships, damaging the social expectations of the child. Domination and control as viable components of interpersonal relationships are then internalized and become part of the fabric of these children's worldview (Graham-Bermann, 1998).

In these families, children at all ages are likely to develop distorted relationships with their parents, both the abuser and the abused. These relationships are likely to need to be a focus of intervention. The abused parent is likely to have one coping strategy for the violence, whether it is to shield the children from the violence, thereby creating an atmosphere of family secrets, or to be emotionally inaccessible and disengaged from the children, or to be emotionally distraught and rely on the children for support. The abusive parent, too, will have a distorted relationship with the child along much the same continuum. In addition, as previously noted, many abusive parents also abuse their children. When the abuse stops and the parent either remains in the home or leaves, these relationships still need to be addressed. Whether the child sees the abuser determines a great deal of the approach to be taken.

The age of the child is a major factor in exploring the specific impact of spouse abuse on the child. Current research has examined the impact on three groups of children primarily: preschoolers, children 6 to 12, and teenagers. As each age group has specific developmental tasks, the area of impact and the focus of the research have varied with the ages of the children.

Young Children (Preschoolers). Young children are learning to master self-regulation, perceptions of safety, and personal competence. They look to their parents for reassurance, protection, and comfort. Due to the circumstances of the violence itself, parents involved in spouse abuse are likely to have great difficulty meeting these emotional developmental needs, and the attachment process is likely to be disrupted with either or both parents. The parenting demands of young children can easily become the focus of the content of the abuse. In addition, children within this age group are still acquiring major communication skills and are the least likely to be able to communicate their needs and concerns. From their egocentric perspective, they are likely to blame themselves for their own unhappiness and also be frightened at their inability to find safety in the environment.

School-Aged Children (Ages 6-12). School-aged children are beginning to develop some independent activities. However, they still rely on parents for transportation and such, and many of these children become isolated from their peer groups. Such children may be afraid to bring friends home or discouraged from doing so. The violence is a major family secret and impinges on any relationships children are likely to form as they hide the reality from peers and other adult sources of support. Children of this age are learning conflict resolution strategies and the nature of relationships with others. In families where couple's violence is common, both physical and psychological abuse result in distorted perceptions of the nature of relationships and impaired development of social skills, particularly in the area of conflict resolution. In addition, perceptions of threat and emotional safety are distorted, resulting in impaired levels of emotional security. Children of this age lack the resources to effectively escape the environment. With successful escape not available as an option, they often become entangled in the parental dispute or respond with their own acts of misbehavior (males) and emotional withdrawal or somatic complaints (females).

Adolescents (Teenagers). Adolescents tend to focus more on peer groups with less influence placed on parents. Teens, unlike younger children, often do have the resources to escape from witnessing the violence by going to their peer group. However, where can teens go in the middle of the night without disclosing their reason for leaving their home? Research has explored the impact of spouse abuse on teens' relationships with their peers (Levendosky et al., 2002). Results indicate that teens who have witnessed abuse are more prone to delinquent behavior, to relationships with the opposite sex, and to other acts that indicate they are out setting their own rules without the wisdom to avoid the negative consequences (Wolfe & Korsch, 1994). Sometimes older children will instead choose to stay in the home and take on the nurturing role of the parent, seeking to assure the safety of the younger siblings and thereby relinquishing the meeting of their personal needs to escape the violence (Wolfe & Korsch, 1994). Teens who stay in the home may act to stop the violence and subsequently become victims of the parental abuse.

EMOTIONAL DISTURBANCES

Psychological disturbances previously identified in children who witness abuse include disturbances of conduct and disturbances of mood. Children were believed to become more aggressive and oppositional or more withdrawn and depressed. Currently, diagnostically the focus is more toward symptoms consistent with Posttraumatic Stress Disorder and Delinquency (Arroyo & Eth, 1995; Zuckerman et al., 1995).

Children who witness abuse develop symptoms consistent with trauma including the reexperiencing of traumatic arousal and anxiety when exposed to similar stimuli or avoidance (Arroyo & Eth, 1995). It is critical to note that children do *not* become desensitized to their parents' violence (Davies & E. M. Cummings, 1998). Instead, research strongly indicates that children's responses are more similar to those of trauma victims with heightened arousal and increased reactivity (Bevan & Higgins, 2002). Children from homes where physical conflict is present between parents may be more likely to react in a manner that has an impact on their experience of the violence, including leaving the room, taking sides, becoming sad or frightened, or misbehaving when observing conflict between parents.

Children are likely to experience a variety of symptoms of emotional disturbance that are congruent with the perspective that they themselves are victims of trauma. Children often demonstrate agitated rather than withdrawn symptoms of depression. Children who are traumatized are likely to have short attention spans, express emotional insecurity, and express anger that is inconsistent with their immediate surroundings. So far research has yet to identify the specific characteristics of the experience of violence that correspond to the specific symptomatology in the child (Grych et al., 2000). A major difficulty in treating such symptoms is the likelihood of the children encountering the abusive parent again. As noted throughout this volume, abuse accompanies a variety of verbal and nonverbal controlling behaviors. Encountering the abusive parent before significantly addressing the trauma can be experienced by the child as revisiting the traumatic encounters. As with other forms of trauma, the child victim may not experience symptomatology until much later in development. The concerns for "sleeper effects" of abuse are becoming significant (Levendosky et al., 2002). Such effects could include disturbed or distorted relationships with members of the opposite sex, impaired development of social skills at later stages of development, and reexperience of traumatic symptoms such as anxiety at such times as dating in adolescence. Sleeper effects are an important component of any assessment. Even if the abuse occurred early in the child's life, inquiring about and addressing the experience is an important component of any assessment.

Delinquency is associated with abuse in the home, particularly among adolescents. As noted previously, children from such homes are likely to look elsewhere to get their emotional needs met, including their need for emotional closeness and security. In addition, they may spend excessive amounts of time with peers and substantial time unsupervised. They may lose respect for and express a lack of trust in both parents and most adults. Circumstances surrounding the delinquent behavior when it occurs, as well as, more importantly, the adolescent's emotional needs, must be assessed before beginning treatment. A strong caution is needed to avoid diagnosing such adolescents as conduct disordered or labeling them as delinquent. Such labeling is likely to misdirect treatment toward the behavior and insufficiently address the underlying trauma and emotional developmental impairments discussed earlier.

As noted earlier, children who witness abuse, particularly psychological abuse or the psychological component of physical abuse, may develop similar coping strategies in relationships. These coping strategies may be perceived as learned sociopathy including failing to experience empathy in interpersonal relationships. Such behaviors as demeaning, humiliating, or threatening others, lying, and other acts of emotional cruelty are important to assess and may be among the most difficult to address.

Apply these findings to a clinical example: The following is a sample from an initial interview. Charley in this case is 7 years old.

Therapist: I wanted to spend a few minutes getting to know you better. What do you like to do when you're not in school? What's your favorite TV program?

Charley: (responds)

Therapist: Do you have any friends?

Charley: (nods)

Therapist: Who is your best friend?

Charley: (responds)

Therapist: Your Mom seems pretty concerned about you. She says the teacher said you're not paying attention in school, kind of daydreaming. Do you like school? . . . When your mind wan-

	ders, and you don't pay attention, what are you thinking about?
Charley:	I don't know . . . nothin'. . . .
Therapist:	Everybody's thinking about something; are you thinking about not being in school . . . being home . . . about your parents?
Charley:	Sometimes. . . .
Therapist:	Lots of kids think about their parents. Which one do you worry about the most?
Charley:	My Mom. . . .
Therapist:	Why's that? Why do you worry more about your Mom than your Dad?
Charley:	I worry about my Dad too but my Dad's strong . . . I don't know. . . .
Therapist:	Yeah, he is big and strong . . . does he scare you?
Charley:	Sometimes. . . .
Therapist:	When does he scare you?
Charley:	When he yells. . . .
Therapist:	Does he yell a lot?
Charley:	Yeah, but more at my Mom than me and my little brother. . . .
Therapist:	Your Dad yells at your Mom a lot . . . What do you do?
Charley:	I take my little brother and we hide in the room. I don't want to hear it.
Therapist	It sounds pretty scary! Are you taking care of your brother?
Charley:	Yeah. He's little and he cries.
Therapist:	What else are you afraid of?
Charley:	That Daddy might get mad 'cause my brother's crying.
Therapist:	Are you afraid your Dad might hit your brother?
Charley:	Yeah, or hurt Mom more 'cause my brother is crying.
Therapist:	Does he do that?
Charley:	Yeah, sometimes.
Therapist:	Do you worry about this in school?
Charley:	Yeah, they've been fighting a lot lately. . . .
Therapist:	Yelling and stuff?
Charley:	Yeah. . . .
Therapist:	Are you in the room?
Charley:	Sometimes . . . I can always hear them through the wall. . . .
Therapist:	What do you hear?
Charley:	She tells him she's going to leave and . . . (stops, becomes quiet).

Therapist:	What is it?
Charley:	Nothin'. . . .
Therapist:	I bet you're afraid of telling on Dad. . . .
Charley:	Sorta. . . .
Therapist:	Charley, you can really help your family by telling what goes on. What happens when your Dad gets really angry? Does your Dad ever get so mad, he gets violent?
Charley:	(hesitating) Sometimes. . . .
Therapist:	What happens?
Charley:	(hesitating) One time. . . .
Therapist:	Yes?
Charley:	. . . he pushed my Mom down, and he hit her head. When I came out she said she fell.

At this point you can explore the violence in greater detail. Specifics are important, particularly concerning the frequency and severity of the abuse. Is the violence daily; were weapons used; did the child observe marks on the mother the day after the violence occurred? Also, what did the mother do to resolve the violence? Did she ever go to the hospital? Did she go to a shelter? Did she contact relatives or friends? You need to reassure the child that you will attempt to help the family. Often children perceive themselves as somehow responsible for the father's anger, or responsible for protecting the mother. If divorce or separation is imminent, the child may take on the responsibility for the ultimate breakup of the family.

Early intervention is critical. Assessing a child who is brought in for therapy when spousal abuse is suspected should always include direct questioning of the parents about the occurrence of violence in the home. Working with the mother to help educate her to the negative effects on the child of viewing spousal abuse will not only serve to empower the woman, but may also give her the additional motivation she needs to remove herself and her children from an abusive situation.

A LAST WORD ON ASSESSMENT

In this chapter, we have been discussing how the clinician might assess for the existence of violence in intact families. Part of the task of the therapist, however, is to assess for the long-term impact of domestic violence even where an intact family does not present for treatment. Consequently, part of any good assessment should be the evaluation of the context: Which members of the family present for therapy, who is being treated, and what constitutes the family? Although a couple may be divorced, if the father still has ongoing contact with his children during visitation, treatment should consider whether he remains a danger to the family and what impact he continues to have on individual and family functioning. As a result, treatment of family members must consider the father's role even if he is not physically present in the therapy room. Moreover, in many cases, the husband's disappearance from the scene may not by itself signal the end of symptoms caused by his abuse. Family members should be assessed for Posttraumatic Stress Disorder or other long-term consequences of abuse.

4

Treatment of
Spouse Abuse

THE INDIVIDUAL WOMAN

As noted in Chapter 3, the battered woman rarely comes into treatment presenting with battering as her primary concern. Helping the client identify the parameters of the violence she is experiencing can be a useful introductory phase of therapy. Therapy with the individual woman may continue with crisis intervention, short-term therapy, and long-term therapy (see Table 3, "Overview of a Treatment Model for Working With Battered Women," p. 62).

CRISIS INTERVENTION

The first major goal of treatment with battered women is always to address issues of safety. The safety of the woman and her children must be ensured before any additional interventions can occur. Crisis intervention may also include addressing practical issues such as finances, housing, and legal assistance.

Crisis intervention and the development of a safety plan must begin with the first session, as often battered women do not return for additional treatment (Goodstein & Page, 1981). Therefore, you must address safety within this first session as if circumstances will prevent the client from returning for additional treatment. Some clients are at particular risk for battering which may attain lethal proportions (see Table 4, "Assessing for Lethality," p. 63).

Safety plans are of two types: those implemented to keep a woman and her children safe during the violent eruption but not intended to lead to permanent separation, and those intended to keep a woman safe once she has decided to leave her husband permanently.

TABLE 3:

Overview of a Treatment Model for Working With Battered Women

Phase I — Crisis Intervention

    A. Assess for the existence of violence.
    B. Assess the danger the woman is in.
    C. Educate the woman about battering and domestic violence and validate her experience.
    D. Develop and practice a safety or danger-management plan.

Phase II — Short-Term Counseling

    A. Work on empowerment issues.
    B. Develop independent living skills and attitudes.
    C. Help client grieve the loss of the idealized relationship.

Phase III — Long-Term Counseling

    A. Heal the past.
    B. Develop trust.
    C. Work from a trauma recovery model to heal resulting psychological problems.

It is important to note that the goal of the therapist in working with a battered woman must NOT be to get her to leave her violent partner. Most battered women are not interested in leaving their partners but instead want help in getting the violence to stop. Battered women often choose not to return to clinicians who are overly invested in getting them to leave. In addition, a goal of treatment is empowering the woman. The therapist's investment in her leaving is communicated to the woman and serves to further disempower her.

Whether the client chooses to stay in or leave her relationship, safety planning is one of the most important aspects of treating a battered women.

You should help the client develop a safety plan if she has not developed one of her own. The major goal of a safety plan is to decrease the likelihood that the woman will be physically harmed during the next violent episode. Providing safety may include teaching her techniques to deescalate her partner's violence while ensuring that she does not feel responsible for his violence. In addition, a safety plan may include establishing recognizable criteria for physically leaving the batterer's pres-

TABLE 4:

Assessing for Lethality

Key factors to assess in determining whether the batterer has the potential to kill:

- Threats of homicide or suicide
- Acute depression and hopelessness
- Possession of weapons
- Obsessiveness about partner or family; beliefs that he cannot live without them or that they are the center of his universe
- Rage
- Drug or alcohol consumption combined with despair
- History of pet abuse
- Easy access to the battered woman and/or family members

The presence of the preceding indicators increases the likelihood that the batterer is contemplating killing or committing life-endangering violence.

ence temporarily when he is violent. Some of the elements of the safety plan (Register, 1993) may include discussion of the following:

1. How to predict that violence is imminent
2. How to physically leave the situation (i.e., identification and rehearsal of an exit route)
3. Exploration of whether safety is best provided by a brief or more lengthy departure
4. Preparation of a safety kit that includes items necessary for survival upon departure (e.g., clothing, medication, money, car keys) to be kept near the exit route
5. Arrangements for shelter, lodging, or friends who will provide a safe haven (in all instances, the shelter arrangements should be made so that the batterer will not know of the woman's whereabouts)

Many therapists working with battered women tell of the creative safety plans of their clients who decide to permanently leave their partners: A battered woman might slowly and gradually remove vital items from the home over a period of weeks or months. Then, the day she finally leaves, she is completely prepared to begin a new life with all the necessary economic and physical resources. She may also choose to leave a note or a message on the answering machine rather than speak to her partner directly.

You should proceed with caution if your client is intent on permanently leaving the batterer. Many batterers threaten to kill their wife if she leaves, and this threat needs to be taken seriously because the risk of death increases when the battered woman leaves her abuser (Browne, 1987). In addition, men who kill their wives and then themselves are more likely to do so during the period of separation or divorce (Price & Hansen, 1991). Therefore, if the client's partner threatens that he will kill himself if she were to leave, she must be concerned for her own safety as well as the safety of her children. Keeping a woman safe when she leaves a batterer is a difficult task.

Most battered women who leave the batterer return to him and are then at greater risk of injury. The battered woman who eventually leaves returns six to seven times on average before she makes her final move (Browne, 1987). You must be careful not to have overinvested in the client's leaving. Also, you may fail to engage and retain clients if your first recommendation is that the woman terminate her relationship. The client may perceive you as not recognizing the positive characteristics in the relationship and her emotional needs for the relationship. In addition, she may perceive you as judgmental and thinking less of her for experiencing the emotional needs that keep her in the relationship. Because some clients report violence occurring at some point in their relationship and later subsiding, ensuring the client's safety does not always mean helping the client leave her partner.

Beyond providing for the client's safety, crisis counseling also serves to help the battered woman realize that you are taking her circumstances seriously. This is particularly important because her defensive style may be to minimize her perceptions of the seriousness and potential dangerousness of her environment. Your intervention can help her examine the specific characteristics of her circumstances while together you strategize safer alternatives. Moreover, because her self-esteem may be so diminished that she is not able to conceptualize functional alternatives, she may need your assistance to begin the process of rebuilding her perceptions of self-worth.

SHORT-TERM COUNSELING

The second goal of therapy is to help the woman identify the impact of the violence on her emotional functioning. Some clients report symptoms consistent with Posttraumatic Stress Disorder (PTSD). These clients are not likely to recognize the basis for their emotional symptoms, and their partners may use these symptoms to further maintain control in the relationship. For example, battered women often report their partners telling them they are emotionally unstable, crazy, or overreacting. Physicians may prescribe medication for the treatment of stress and anxiety, further supporting the client's perception of her emotional disorder. A diagnosis such as PTSD or Adjustment Disorder may help the client externalize the basis for her symptoms and help her to become an expert on her own reactions to stress. Attributing the symptoms to the battering rather than to the woman's own traits may be most effective with clients who are inclined to request reading material from you. Recognizing the specific precipitant and the predictable pattern of anxiety or depressive reactions can help to increase your client's sense of personal control.

Empowerment is a major goal in working with women who have been battered. Battering is currently conceptualized as a batterer's method of controlling his partner. The client, therefore, has been functioning in a relationship with little personal power or control over her circumstances. Therapy, then, focuses on helping her to regain her sense of personal independence and on helping her shift from focusing on her partner to focusing on her own needs. You can also help the client explore personal resources she may not recognize or may have abandoned at the demand of her partner. Battered women often become increasingly isolated from peers and sources of emotional support. Therefore, you can encourage the client to gradually explore reconnecting with the people she perceives as supportive to her. The client's safety remains paramount in all interventions. You must be cautious when recommending that the client work to change her current environment if these changes are perceived by her as conflicting with the wishes of her partner. If the client does not feel safe in pursuing the specific recommendations, you need to respect her sense of caution.

LONG-TERM COUNSELING

You can also help the client address the concerns of the past. Clients often feel a need to address their contributions to the conflict in their relationships. Contributions to conflict can be explored while creating distinctions between verbal conflict, and emotional control and physical abuse. You can help the client recognize that her feelings of guilt and responsibility for the problems in the relationship are often a function of the abuse of the relationship and not the cause of the abuse, as her partner has maintained.

In the later stages of therapy you can help the client explore alternatives for the future. Helping the client examine her resources and acquire new skills increases her sense of power in her life. Often clients who are battered are emotionally drained and entirely preoccupied with the primary relationship. After the immediate danger is addressed, the client may begin to be ready to expand her perceptions of life's possibilities. Helping the client to open new doors can be an additional source of empowerment for her.

Several cautions are needed in working with women who have been battered. You must examine your own political beliefs and feelings about spouse abuse. Particular sensitivity is required in working with the woman who chooses to stay with an abusive partner. In addition, you need to be careful to speak respectfully of her partner to the client, because clients are emotionally involved with the partner, regardless of the wisdom of that involvement. You need to be sensitive to this emotional attachment and any feelings that may remain. You also need to be sensitive to your own comfort with discussions of the violence. The client may want to speak in graphic detail about her physical or sexual abuse. However, she is only likely to discuss the abuse as long as you are comfortable with the discussion.

Case Example: Catherine. Catherine is a 38-year-old mother of two adolescent daughters. She is in the process of separating from her husband of 20 years. She has come to the therapist at the recommendation of her attorney to help her with parenting skills and to facilitate her positive presentation in court. During the first session, Catherine describes feelings of intense anxiety and fear. She also states she frequently loses her temper at her daughters and is afraid she is a poor parent. Her description of her marriage reveals a pattern of humiliation and manipulation on the part of her husband. Further, she describes her last contact with him at the time of a regularly scheduled visitation with their daughters. He had entered the house to examine some medical insurance forms. They began to argue about responsibility for the deductible. She believes he was trying to renege on his responsibility, using as an excuse that she had not called him before taking her daughter to the emergency room. Catherine states she then asked him to leave but he persisted in arguing. She says she placed her hand on his back to guide him to the door. He flung her arm off and in the process whacked her across the face. The bruise is still visible from the altercation. She states she has been feeling anxious since that time and experiencing panic attacks. She acknowledges having difficulty sleeping and having dreams about prior altercations.

The Therapy. Early on, the therapist inquires about Catherine's future contact with her husband and finds that Catherine has been advised by her attorney to never see her husband without another adult present. The therapist inquires about her husband's treatment of the daughters and is told they protect each other from his psychological manipulation. The therapist, then, interviews Catherine about other possible symptoms and discovers Catherine appears to be suffering from PTSD. She shares this observation with her client and helps normalize the symptoms: "You're not going crazy, this is a very common response to these circumstances. You might expect to feel . . . at times during the coming week." Catherine asks for literature on PTSD and is referred to a support group at a local shelter. Future sessions focus on helping Catherine rebuild her life and reestablish her self-confidence.

ESTABLISHING GOALS IN WORKING WITH BATTERED WOMEN

The following list is offered to assist you in establishing goals for treatment with battered women (Register, 1993):

- *Identification of the Impact of Violence on Functioning.* Clients adjust their entire life to avoid the violence of the spouse. Recognition of the specific alterations and accommodations of behavior are an important component of treatment.
- *Empowerment.* Helping clients shift from a self-perception as victims to individuals who are in charge of their own lives is a slow but important process.
- *Development of Problem-Solving Skills.* Clients need to develop and enhance their skills both in daily living and in interacting with the social agencies that will help improve their circumstances.
- *Interacting With Social Agencies.* Battering brings women into contact with the legal system and many social service agencies. Battered women often become single women and single parents when they separate from their abusive partner. The largest percentage of persons below the poverty level are female single parents, and a majority of women experience a major reduction in income following divorce. Battered women need to learn to obtain the public help that is available to them.
- *Providing Ongoing Support for Battered Women.* Battered women often benefit from support groups that occur concurrently with ongoing psychotherapy.

THERAPY FOR THE BATTERER

Batterers rarely receive treatment voluntarily. They may present in your office seeking help for their spouse. "There's something wrong with my wife, doctor, fix her." Or, you may recognize a batterer during the initial phone request for couple's therapy. An abusive man may focus almost entirely on the negative characteristics of his partner during this initial contact. Or, he may come to treatment with his spouse when one of the children develops problems. In any case, spousal abuse assessment skills will be particularly important for you to develop (see also Table 5, "Checklist of Physical Violence Predispositions," p. 69).

Men who batter are best referred to programs for batterers because therapy for abusive men is most effectively provided by batterers' programs and in group therapy. Reviews of individual treatments suggest that individual counseling is most effective when provided as a supplemental service to group treatment (Gondolf, 1993). Individual sessions with abusive men might also help them to recognize the potential benefits available to them in attending batterer treatment programs. These programs can provide emotional support and help batterers acquire alternative strategies for getting their needs met. Moreover, as noted in Chapter 3, not all batterers present with the same psychological profile, and interventions may need to be tailor-made for their needs. For instance, some violent men have drug or alcohol problems and need to receive *simultaneous* treatment for the substance abuse (Cooley, 1993). On the other hand, some batterers have antisocial personalities and are not likely to be responsive to any treatment approach.

The scope of existing treatment programs for batterers varies greatly from programs that focus on anger management, often in a psychoeducational format, to programs that are more psychotherapeutic in their approach. Many treatment programs incorporate elements of the Duluth model (Pence & McDonnell, 2000), which can be described as "feminist socioeducational." Other approaches involve cognitive-behavioral interventions, feminist psychodynamic interventions, or narrative approaches. The length of the interventions varies from 12 weeks (Sonkin & Durphy, 1989) to 52 weeks in probation-mandated programs in California.

Recognizing that not all batterers are alike suggests that not all batterers should be treated in the same way. The reality, however, is that at the treatment level, there is very little attempt to assess different kinds of batterers and orient them to different kinds of treatment. Gelles (1998) suggests using Prochaska and DiClemente's Transtheoretical Model of Change (Prochaska & DiClemente, 1992) as an element in determining

---

TABLE 5:

Checklist of
Physical Violence Predispositions*

1.	Unreasonable jealousy
2.	Controlling behavior, initially presented as for the woman's safety and well-being
3.	Quick involvement and pressure to make a quick commitment
4.	Unrealistic expectations that the partner will meet all of his needs
5.	Isolation or cutting the woman off from all resources
6.	Blaming others for all his problems
7.	Blaming others for his feelings
8.	Hypersensitivity: easily insulted or hurt
9.	Cruelty to animals and children
10.	"Playful" use of force in sex
11.	Verbal abuse
12.	Rigid sex roles
13.	Dr. Jekyll and Mr. Hyde: abrupt mood changes
**14.	Past battering
**15.	Threats of violence (e.g., "I'll beat the hell out of you")
**16.	Breaking or striking objects, especially prized possessions
**17.	Use of any force during an argument

*Modified with permission from materials developed by the Project for Victims of Family Violence, Inc., Fayetteville, Arkansas.
**These factors are almost always predictive of battering.

---

what type of intervention might be most effective. The Transtheoretical Model of Change examines the individual's predisposition to make the necessary change. The stages include the Precontemplation Stage, where the individual has no intention of changing the problem behavior. He may, in fact, be unaware that the behavior needs changing, may react defensively when confronted about the problem behavior, and may suggest that it is the behavior of others around him that must change. When the severity of risk is also assessed as high, Gelles indicates that this individual would probably not benefit from treatment and should instead be incarcerated. Other stages of readiness for change include Contemplation (awareness of the problem, thoughts about change, but little commitment to change), Preparation (setting goals and priorities for change; readiness to change within a short period of time), Action (modification of the problem behavior over short periods of time and commitment of time and energy toward consolidating the change), and Maintenance (consolidation of changes of the earlier stages; relapse prevention planning). Gelles also suggests that it is with these later stages of change that formal intervention programs may be more effective.

The majority of programs for batterers recognize a spectrum of violence (Gondolf, 1993; see also Table 6, "Identifying Domestic Violence," p. 71). Such programs address the concern that the threat of violence often continues in homes where physical violence has stopped. Spouse abuse is recognized not as a response to anger but more often as a strategy utilized to maintain power in the relationship. This position of power is regarded as the man's entitlement. He retains this sense of entitlement through self-pity, denial, rationalization, manipulation, and general disregard for his partner. These characteristics are difficult, if not impossible, to challenge in individual therapy. Therefore, skilled group leadership is required for effective treatment.

Current evaluation of treatment programs suggests that treatment often requires long-term intervention of 18 months to 2 years (although, as noted above, most group programs are considerably shorter). Often the physical violence is reduced, but the verbal threats and control require more intensive intervention (Gondolf, 1993).

The course of therapy with men who batter and who have reached some minimum awareness of the problematic nature of this behavior could also be conceptualized as consisting of three phases which parallel the treatment phases for the battered woman. It is important to consider that the batterer, too, may feel powerless in his interactions with his partner. His feeling of powerlessness expresses itself in greater efforts to control the woman and eventually in greater violence. For him, the major treatment goal will be to help him identify his feelings of vulnerability and learn to channel these in socially appropriate ways (see Table 7, "Batterer Treatment Model Overview," p. 72).

CRISIS INTERVENTION

The crisis intervention phase will include teaching him about violence, the cycle of violence, and the fact that he alone is responsible for the cycle. He also needs to be taught that abuse is often a defense against feelings (see also Table 2, "The Cycle of Feeling Avoidance," p. 45). Learning to identify the feelings that are defended against is primary. Treatment will then consist of more socially acceptable channeling of these feelings into exercise, sports, or an acknowledgment of vulnerabilities to the partner. The development of a danger-management plan is also key early in treatment. The danger-management plan focuses on teaching

---

TABLE 6:

Identifying Domestic Violence*

Domestic Violence may include any of the following:

I. Physical Violence – using one's physical strength or presence to *control* someone

    A. Pushing or shoving

    B. Slapping, grabbing, biting, hitting, spanking, kicking

    C. Holding down, twisting arms, banging head on floor, choking, pinning against wall, carrying against her will

    D. Forced sex

    E. Kneeing, hair pulling, punching

    F. Burning, trying to run over with car

    G. Throwing objects, punching walls or doors, breaking windshields

    H. Breaking or tearing clothes and personal objects

    I. Driving recklessly to scare

    J. Blocking exits or car, taking keys, taking money or bank cards – all to prevent her from leaving

    K. Unplugging the phone

II. Verbal and Emotional Abuse – using one's words or voice to *control* someone

    A. Coercion and threats, including threatening divorce, suicide, reporting her to the authorities, making her do illegal things

    B. Intimidation, including making her afraid by using looks, actions, and gestures

    C. Stalking or checking up on her, accusations of sexual infidelity

    D. Isolation, including controlling her activities and possessions (e.g., access to the phone, interrogations about her activities, preventing her from seeing friends or family, intense jealousy)

    E. Economic abuse including preventing her from working or going to school, controlling the finances

    F. Threatening or using the children (e.g., making her feel guilty about the children, threatening to take the children)

    G. Invoking male privilege (e.g., treating her like a servant, making all the decisions, defining roles, being master of the castle)

    H. Emotional abuse (e.g., putdowns, name-calling, denigration, mind games)

---

*Adapted and modified with permission from materials developed by the Domestic Abuse Intervention Project, Duluth, Minnesota.

---

the batterer self-control (Segel-Evans, 1991). It involves identifying a list of trigger points, situations, or feelings likely to result in abuse (e.g., "I can't stand it when. . . ."), a list of personal signals that a dangerous

TABLE 7:

Batterer Treatment
Model Overview

Phase I   – Crisis Intervention

    A.   Educate about violence and violence control
    B.   Help with the identification of feelings
    C.   Teach socially acceptable channeling of feelings
    D.   Develop a danger-management plan

Phase II – Short-Term Counseling

    A.   Channel power needs into socially acceptable channels
    B.   Shame and guilt work
    C.   Explore fears of abandonment

Phase III – Long-Term Counseling

    A.   Heal abuse of the past
    B.   Develop relational skills with other men, women, and spouse

situation is developing (e.g., bodily sensations, the appearance of fear in his partner, etc.), a list of steps or techniques to reduce the danger (e.g., time out, positive self-talk, etc.), and a list of steps to reduce the danger over time.

SHORT-TERM AND LONG-TERM COUNSELING

Short-term counseling issues involve teaching the batterer ways to rechannel his needs for power into more socially acceptable ways of getting his more basic needs met. Batterers often externalize the blame for the things that happen to them. Unlike other groups who suffer consciously and unreasonably from shame and guilt, many batterers are not aware of these feelings, although they may be at the root of violent outbursts. A goal of short-term counseling may be to examine the existence of these feelings and also those related to fears of abandonment, which often also underlie violent outbursts.

Longer term counseling issues may consider healing the abuse of the past (because many batterers were themselves abused) and helping them develop successful relational skills.

Case Example: Mark. Mark, a 39-year-old chef in a successful restaurant, has come in for an intake interview. He seems confused about why he has been referred for counseling, although he does mention that the district attorney told him he must be in counseling. Upon further probing, the therapist learns that Mark held his wife Sarah on the bed when she threatened leaving him. Only after considerable additional probing does it become clear that the police were called by Mark and Sarah's neighbors who overhead her screams. They arrived to find Sarah with multiple bruises and lacerations and a broken nose. Mark claims that he only held her down on the bed and does not know how Sarah's injuries occurred. The couple have been married 5 years, Sarah is pregnant with their second child, and they have a history of increasingly more violent arguments. Mark claims that this was the first time that things had gotten serious enough for the police to be called. He tells the therapist that Sarah was very sweet when they first met, but that over the last 2 years, she had become increasingly more defiant. She had been wanting to return to work (she is trained as a nurse) but he tells the therapist, "No wife of mine will work as long as I am healthy enough to earn a living." The couple emigrated from Israel shortly after their marriage and have no family or friends in this country.

The Therapy. In working with Mark, the therapist will need to teach him about the cycle of violence and help him accept responsibility for his actions. Learning to identify the feelings that lead to his outbursts and learning how to channel them into more acceptable ways will be paramount. Over the long term, Mark's own family-of-origin issues will need to be explored.

THERAPY WITH THE COUPLE

As long as the man is violent, couple's therapy is not recommended. Instead, with most couples, each member should be treated separately: the man in a batterers' group with individual therapy as adjunctive and the woman in individual therapy with additional support from a group for battered women. Couple's therapy should begin only when the violence has stopped and preferably when each member of the couple has received treatment separately.

BEGINNING COUPLE'S THERAPY:
TREATMENT GOALS

Once the violence has ceased, the primary goal of couple's therapy is to help the couple establish new patterns of relating. The relationship of couples where violence has existed is usually founded on power and control. The man is afraid of losing his control or is unwilling to share control with his spouse. Your role as therapist is to begin to modify patterns of communication that serve to maintain the negative qualities of the relationship. Both partners must begin to recognize the benefit in mutual sharing of power and must acknowledge that in any relationship no one wins if one person loses.

A positive focus of treatment can be to help the couple reconnect with the qualities in each other that were the initial foundation of the relationship. Most couples can begin to identify the positive qualities that attracted them to each other. In addition, most couples can recall times when they enjoyed each other and did not fight. The oft-quoted saying "The opposite of love is not hate but indifference" is often true for couples who choose to stay together after the violence has stopped. Helping the couple identify the love in the relationship provides the therapist with the flexibility to explore more difficult topics.

Many batterers have emotional vulnerabilities in addition to the proclivity for violence. These vulnerabilities are often hidden by the violent behavior and the need to control the relationship through manipulation or violence. Couple's therapy may provide the opportunity to explore these vulnerabilities with the partner in the presence of a safe outsider. You need to protect both members of the couple as these vulnerabilities and hidden concerns are explored. The battered woman is likely to continue to feel anger toward her spouse and may feel a desire to direct this anger toward him as he exposes this softer side of himself. The batterer is likely to have difficulty acknowledging these concerns and may minimize or be quick to terminate the exploration. You are responsible for monitoring the process and ensuring the safety of both clients during the sessions and after they leave your office.

LATER THERAPY: TREATMENT GOALS

You are also responsible for helping clients acquire new skills of conflict resolution. Differences of opinion are present in all relationships. Few couples are skilled at mutually discussing and resolving their differences. You can help the couple explore new strategies and maintain the level of emotional intensity so as to allow good work to take place. Conflict resolution may be approached later in the course of therapy after trust has had an opportunity to be reestablished in the relationship.

Several cautions are needed for therapists who are working with couples where violence has occurred. First, as with any therapy, the safety of the clients is paramount. If at any time you believe that your own safety or the safety of either client cannot be ensured, therapy should be terminated and other safety precautions undertaken. Second, it is critical that you be perceived as mutually supportive and not aligned with either member of the couple. The purpose of couple's therapy is to help develop a mutually supportive relationship that benefits both members. It is also possible that, through the course of therapy, one or the other partner may begin to recognize they are no longer invested in the relationship and decide they would like to separate from their partner. At this point, the direction of therapy would change and the focus might be toward a safe dissolution of the relationship. Third, you must be aware of your own political beliefs and refrain from allowing these beliefs to influence the course of treatment. When the therapist approaches the couple with caution and sensitivity, therapy can help couples who wish to stay together develop more functional and supportive relationships.

Case Example: Joe and Bonnie. Joe and Bonnie have come to therapy for help with their marriage. Joe has called the therapist and reports his wife has become extensively involved in the Parent/Teachers Association (PTA). As a consequence, he is afraid the family is suffering. The therapist agrees to see the couple. Both partners come to the initial session. Bonnie admits that, now that the children are in school, she has become very active in the PTA. However, when Joe first indicated he felt this was having an impact on the family, she agreed to reduce her involvement and consider counseling. Joe and Bonnie have been married for 15 years. They have three children, ages 10, 11, and 13. The children reportedly do well in school and are involved in local sporting activities. Bonnie indicates that she has been very involved in the children's school and extracurricular activities during the past 3 years. Prior to that time, she stayed at home. Joe indicates Bonnie has not worked since their marriage. "I think a mother should be home with the children," he states. The couple describes positive experiences prior to the birth of the children. Activities revolved around Joe's friends and the many parties and afternoon cookouts the couple attended. Bonnie reports Joe began to drink more at these parties after their first child was born. Joe retorts that everyone drank. Bonnie indicates that she started to stay home with the children rather than go to the parties and states that Joe would often be driven home by his friends because he was too drunk to drive. She also indicates that when she complained about the drinking he lashed out and pushed her away. She admits she was afraid of her husband and feels angry that she was made to feel afraid. Both members of the couple agree drinking is no longer a problem. Joe stopped drinking when he received a DUI 3 years ago and lost his license for 6 months. Both members of the couple agree they don't feel as close to each other as they did when they were first married. They are particularly concerned with the impact of their differences on the children. Their daughter has been reluctant to leave home to go to school, and they are afraid their conflict might be partially responsible. They both agree that violence in the relationship has stopped. Bonnie acknowledges residual anger but is not currently afraid of her husband.

The Therapy. With this couple, the initial phase of therapy focuses on helping the clients rediscover the joy and pleasure they felt with each other early in the marriage. Therapy also explores what they perceive as the characteristics of a positive mature marriage and how they envision themselves in that role. In therapy, Joe and Bonnie begin to explore characteristics of the earlier relationship, especially those that could be characterized as less mature and more fear-based. The therapist normalizes these fears and places them in an appropriate developmental context. After this positive foundation is established, the couple explores specific areas of conflict in their relationship. The therapist highlights the benefit to both partners of mutual support for individual growth within the relationship.

THERAPY WITH CHILDREN

Far more work has been published on the identification of the emotional and behavioral concerns of children who witness abuse than on treatment approaches with these children. Publication on treatment of children is likely to focus on three modalities: individual treatment approaches, group therapy approaches, and parent/child interventions. By far the most widely written-about approach for children who witness abuse is that of group interventions; the least is parent/child and family interventions (Groves, 1999; Lehmann et al., 1994; Rossman, 1994). However, spouse abuse is most likely to be identified in families when the parent, the victim, appears for treatment rather than the child. Nonetheless, spouse abuse is a family problem when children are members of the family.

INDIVIDUAL TREATMENT APPROACHES

Individual approaches for working with children most often implement a trauma model for intervention (Groves, 1999; Silvern, Karyl, & Landis, 1995). These models focus on the distress the child is experiencing after the traumatic event. The sequence of intervention starts with identification of the traumatic symptoms. Such symptoms include avoidance, numbing, withdrawal; reexperiencing of the event through flashbacks, dreams, or intense distress; hyperarousal, sleep disturbance, and agitation. The subsequent initial intervention facilitates the understanding and connection of the persistent distress to the event, connecting the anxiety to the source with cognitive understanding through talking directly about the events, emotions, and meaning of the events. Next, the intervention focuses on desensitization, cognitive restructuring, and the connections between the events and symptoms. Lastly the intervention focuses on adaptive strategies to cope with these events (Silvern et al., 1995).

GROUP THERAPY APPROACHES

Group therapy approaches are most often conducted with groups of similar-aged children and often take place in shelters or outpatient clinics. Many protocols are published and available for practitioners who would like to adopt such interventions (Groves, 1999). Though the majority of programs target children in the middle years, programs are available for both teens and toddlers (Huth-Bocks, Schettini, & Shebroe, 2001; Peled, 1998; Peled & Edleson, 1995). Such group therapy programs often adopt a psychoeducational approach. The concerns that are addressed are similar, though the content of the interventions are tailored to the specific age of the children. The common concerns include issues of safety and stability in the home. By bringing children together to discuss their common experiences, the large impact of family secrecy is addressed, because the group functionally breaks the family's covert rule of silence. Psycho-educational groups for all ages increase the children's understanding of events. In homes where spouse abuse is present, children receive conflicting messages and emotions and experiences simply do not add up. Group interventions serve to reduce this confusion and clarify the children's experiences. Children learn they are not alone in these experiences and learn to accurately identify and cope with their emotional responses to these traumatic events. Children's impairments in conflict resolution skills may be addressed as well as the impact on their ability to form emotionally empathic relationships with others. Developmental tasks may be the focus of such groups. For example, dating relationships may be explored in adolescent groups.

Most group protocols are time limited from 10 to 14 weeks with specific topics scheduled for each session of about 90 minutes. A typical sequence of topics would include (a) defining the violence and responsibility, (b) expressing feelings, (c) improving communication and coping skills, (d) increasing self-esteem, (e) developing social support, (f) developing safety plans, and (g) increasing feelings of safety and trust. The interventions result in breaking patterns of secrecy, increasing children's ability to protect themselves, increasing self-esteem of children by helping them recognize they are not alone, and creating a safe, positive experience (Peled & Edleson, 1995).

Group interventions may not be the most conducive approach for independent practitioners, especially for those who see only a small number of children. Groups may range in size from three to six children within an age group. Treatment plans and protocols from published programs can serve as useful guidelines of topics to be addressed in more individualized interventions.

PARENT/CHILD INTERVENTIONS

An important focus addressed less frequently than both these approaches is the involvement of mothers and siblings in treatment (Lehmann et al., 1994). The custodial parent (assuming parents have separated) needs to improve his or her relationship with the children. Reestablishing the mother in the role of authority as a parent is often effective in family sessions, which should be considered for the family members that remain together. Helping mothers be in charge of their children without being challenged or being perceived as abusive is important. Having the single parent take on the responsibility of two parents without experiencing guilt for the absence of the abusive spouse is also a critical step in the process. Children need to regain self-confidence as well as regain confidence in their parent. This process might be difficult, particularly when mothers perceive paternal resemblances in their children. Interventions within this context can help the new family develop new rituals and new family patterns. As in other families that have experienced divorce, the economic concerns cannot be overlooked. Clinicians need to help mothers see themselves as single mothers, not just as abused spouses. Often family interventions in addition to individually focused interventions can assist in this process. Mother's roles are strengthened with the children present, and the children's unique characteristics can be identified. The families redefine themselves as providing safe, stable, and nurturing environments with consistent discipline. These interventions become particularly challenging when the father visits and may be even more challenging when the father remains in the home, even though the physical abuse has stopped. Particular caution is needed for the therapist to recognize what may be lingering patterns of psychological abuse under these circumstances. As noted, psychological abuse often takes the form of subtle control through demeaning the spouse, or through symbolic verbalizations, such as a subtle reference to past interpersonal history.

When working with individual clients, either children or their families, the issue of safety and stability needs to be addressed before all others. Intervening on this topic may require the clinician to step outside the more traditional role and advocate for the clients (Hughes & Marshall, 1995). As mentioned earlier, the assessment of the child and family will provide the context for the intervention. Household members will determine many of the concerns that need to be addressed. In independent practice, unlike in the shelter environment, the abusing parent may remain in contact with the child through visitation or may still be in the home.

Case Example: Bill. Bill is a 14 year old living with his mother and sister, Amy, age 10. Bill's mother indicates that she divorced the children's father 2 years ago, after a tumultuous marriage. The children visit their father every other weekend. Amy often becomes ill before the visits and as a result visits him infrequently. Both children acknowledge their father was violent toward their mother. At one time the mother was hospitalized with broken ribs and the family stayed at a shelter for 2 weeks. After this most violent episode, divorce proceedings were begun.

Bill is currently challenging his mother and requesting increased independence. His curfew is 10:00 p.m. on weekends and he wants this extended to "at least 11:00 p.m." He does well in school and is involved in sports. His mother is concerned with his "attitude around the house." She complains that his room is a mess and she has to remind him constantly to complete his chores. She acknowledges she is also concerned with her daughter's clear desire not to visit her father. Bill indicates he has other things he would rather do on weekends as well, but admits that sometimes his father takes him to sporting events, which he enjoys.

The Therapy. After a thorough evaluation, family therapy is initiated. Much of Bill's behavior is normalized as age-appropriate adolescent behavior. Therapy focuses on helping the family develop skills for conflict resolution and compromise. Bill offers to try to help his sister cope with the visits with their father. Positive characteristics of the family are highlighted, particularly Bill's traits that are resourceful and different from his father's. Therapy helps the family unite to formulate creative strategies for containing the weekend visits with the father. The children's feelings of ambivalence and the mother's struggle with these feelings are shared openly among the family members. Therapy also assists the mother in setting limits with Bill; 10:00 is an appropriate time for a 14 year old's curfew. She too offers to help Amy talk about any fears she may experience visiting her father without discussing the mother's marital difficulties. Therapy is relatively short term and terminated with the understanding that further consultation is available if needed.

SUMMARY

The first goal of treatment with the battered woman, the batterer, the couple, and the children is to ensure the safety of the clients. The battering must stop or the clients must leave the battering situation before treatment of the trauma that results from battering can begin. All treatments, therefore, begin with crisis intervention, attention to immediate needs for safety, and problem solving of immediate concerns. The second component of all treatment is to help the clients regain the resources and self-worth that preceded the trauma of the abuse. These resources are needed for the healing process. The battered woman needs to become again the person she once was prior to the loss of self-esteem she experienced as a victim of abuse. The batterer needs to access the resources to control his behavior. The couple, if they are to remain a couple, need to access the positive characteristics and experiences that brought them together and that they have shared throughout their relationship. The children need to explore their own strengths and coping strategies to help them recover from the trauma and fully develop as individuals. Lastly, all clients need to learn to function beyond the battering and discover themselves, their strengths, and their limitations, following the treatment for the trauma of abuse.

5

A Final Word on
Spouse Abuse

This book explores current approaches to the assessment and treatment of spouse abuse. Chapter 1 mentions that spouse abuse occurs in 20% to 50% of the population. Thirty percent to 70% of batterers also abuse their children (Hughes, 1982; Straus, 1980). Clinicians who do not specialize in the treatment of battering have indicated that as much as 60% of their client caseload may have experienced domestic violence. Battering occurs in couples from all ethnic and socioeconomic backgrounds, and alcohol abuse may intensify the likelihood of battering (from 48% to 87% of alcohol abusers are batterers [Cooley, 1993]).

As our self-quiz (Chapter 2) suggests, numerous myths exist about spousal abuse, including:

- definitions of domestic violence (the close relationship between psychological abuse and physical abuse and how spousal abuse manifests)
- the prevalence and seriousness of spousal abuse (much more prevalent and serious than most believe)
- the kind of woman who is battered (any woman) and her responsibility for the violence (the responsibility is always that of the batterer)
- the dynamics of battering (the batterer may have a history of abuse of various kinds but he is likely to be like most men in his personality profile)
- treatment and assessment issues (the need for safety planning and the importance of assessment)

- legal and ethical issues (laws covering therapists and protection provided by the authorities)

In Chapter 3, we emphasized that assessment of spouse abuse requires careful screening of all clients who request therapy. Clients who request treatment from practitioners rarely present spouse abuse as their primary reason for seeking services. Victims of abuse may present with symptoms of depression or anxiety, batterers may seek help for their wives, and children who have witnessed abuse may present with behavioral problems. However, we maintain that battering occurs so frequently that all clients should be assessed for a history of experiencing, committing, or witnessing battering.

The most critical concern in any assessment is the determination of the immediate danger to the client or members of the client's family. The familiar questions of who, what, when, where, and how serve as guidelines in evaluating the frequency and severity of the violence. The therapist should err on the side of thoroughness in conducting the evaluation. Therapists must recognize that many victims of abuse do not return for a second visit; thus, the first visit is the only opportunity to ensure the safety of the client. Work with the couple, the batterer, or the children in families where abuse occurs requires the same thoroughness and the same approach to ensuring safety.

The second component of assessment requires an evaluation of the functioning of the client. What should be examined are the practical and emotional resources available to the client. This should be examined in the case of the battered woman, the batterer, the couple, and the children of the abuse. Assessment of functioning includes cognitive, emotional, and practical factors because these resources will be called upon throughout the intervention.

The therapist must acknowledge that spouse abuse is not socially desirable. Therefore, social expectations may interfere with a client's willingness to disclose violence. Consequently, interviews need to occur individually with each family member to ensure that presence of others in the family does not restrict the amount of self-disclosure. This approach is required when working with all members of the family: with the battered woman, the batterer, and the children. Children may be especially reluctant to disclose the violence in the presence of their parents for fear of appearing disloyal to one of the parents.

In Chapter 4, we detailed treatment issues. Crisis intervention begins during the first stage of treatment and may occur throughout therapy. Safety from abuse and stopping the violence are the two primary considerations. Therapists may need to reconceptualize their traditional role to include helping clients contact social and legal agencies. Batterers may need concurrent treatment at drug and alcohol facilities and batterers' groups. Battered women will also need help interacting with social agencies, because often a consequence of long-term abuse is the inability to deal with practical life situations. Therapists may be required to facilitate the coordination and integration of these services.

Treatment for battering requires long-term intervention. The recovery of battered women and the batterers' acceptance of responsibility for the violence may be a slow process even among motivated clients. Many women return to abusive spouses several times before leaving, and the prognosis for batterers (especially without treatment) is poor. Children, too, may require treatment. Therapists need to be careful not to become discouraged, not to expect rapid change, and to be pleased with small steps toward growth. Recovery can occur, but may require many different visits to many different therapists. Certainly with appropriate treatment, new families can be created once the abuse is no longer present – new families formed with hope and respect.

References

American Psychiatric Association. (1987). *Diagnostic and Statistical Manual of Mental Disorders* (3rd ed. rev.). Washington, DC: Author.

American Psychiatric Association. (1994). *Diagnostic and Statistical Manual of Mental Disorders* (4th ed.). Washington, DC: Author.

Arroyo, W., & Eth, S. (1995). Assessment following violence-witnessing trauma. In E. Peled, P. G. Jaffe, & J. L. Edleson (Eds.), *Ending the Cycle of Violence: Community Responses to Children of Battered Women* (pp. 27-42). Thousand Oaks, CA: Sage.

Bachman, R., & Saltzman, L. E. (1995). *Violence Against Women: Estimates From the Redesigned Survey* (Bureau of Justice Statistics Special Report NCJ 154348). Washington, DC: U.S. Department of Justice.

Barnett, O. W., Miller-Perrin, C. L., & Perrin, R. D. (1997). *Family Violence Across the Lifespan: An Introduction.* Newbury Park, CA: Sage.

Bevan, E., & Higgins, D. J. (2002). Is domestic violence learned? The contribution of five forms of child maltreatment to men's violence and adjustment. *Journal of Family Violence, 17*(3), 223-245.

Bodin, A. M. (1992). *Relationship Conflict Inventory.* Mimeographed instrument. (For additional information, contact Arthur M. Bodin, PhD, 555 Middlefield Road, Palo Alto, CA 94301-2141 or telephone 415-328-3000.)

Briere, J. N., & Runtz, M. (1989). The Trauma Symptom Checklist (TSC-33): Early data on a new scale. *Journal of Interpersonal Violence, 4*, 151-163.

Brown, S. L. (1991). *Counseling Victims of Violence.* Alexandria, VA: American Association for Counseling and Development.

Browne, A. (1987). *When Battered Women Kill.* New York: Free Press.

Burgess, A. W., Hartman, C. R., & Kelly, S. J. (1990). Assessing child abuse: The triads checklist. *Journal of Psychosocial Nursing, 28,* 7-14.

Carlson, B. E. (1984). Children's observations of interparental violence. In A. R. Roberts (Ed.), *Battered Women and Their Families* (pp. 147-167). New York: Springer.

Cervantes, N. N. (1993). Therapist duty in domestic violence cases: Ethical considerations. In M. Hansen & M. Harway (Eds.), *Battering and Family Therapy: A Feminist Perspective* (pp. 147-155). Newbury Park, CA: Sage.

Cheney, A. B., & Bleker, E. G. (1982, August). *Internal-External Locus of Control and Repression-Sensitization in Battered Women.* Paper presented at the annual meeting of the American Psychological Association, Washington, DC.

Connors, J., & Harway, M. (1995). A male-female abuse continuum. *Family Violence and Sexual Assault Bulletin, 11*(1 & 2), 29-33.

Cooley, C. S. (1993). Establishing feminist systemic criteria for viewing violence and alcoholism. In M. Hansen & M. Harway (Eds.), *Battering and Family Therapy: A Feminist Perspective* (pp. 217-226). Newbury Park, CA: Sage.

Cummings, E. M. (1998). Children exposed to marital conflict and violence: Conceptual and theoretical directions. In G. W. Holden, R. Geffner, & E. N. Jouriles (Eds.), *Children Exposed to Marital Violence* (pp. 55-93). Washington, DC: American Psychological Association.

Cummings, E. M., Davies, P. T., & Simpson, K. S. (1994). Marital conflict, gender, and children's appraisals and coping efficacy as mediators of child adjustment. *Journal of Family Psychology, 8*(2), 141-149.

Cummings, J. S., Pellegrini, D. S., Notarius, C. I., & Cummings, E. M. (1989). Children's responses to angry adult behavior as a function of marital distress and history of inter-parent hostility. *Child Development, 60,* 1035-1043.

Davidson, T. (1978). *Conjugal Crime: Understanding and Changing the Wife Beating Pattern.* New York: Hawthorne.

Davies, P. T., & Cummings, E. M. (1998). Exploring children's emotional security as a mediator of the link between marital relations and child adjustment. *Child Development, 69*(1), 124-139.

Dobash, R. E., & Dobash, R. P. (1979). *Violence Against Wives: A Case Against the Patriarchy.* New York: Free Press.

Edleson, J. L., Eisikovits, Z. C., & Guttman, E. (1985). Men who batter women: A critical review of the evidence. *Journal of Family Issues, 6,* 229-247.

Ehrensaft, M. K., & Vivian, D. (1996). Spouses' reasons for not reporting existing marital aggression as a marital problem. *Journal of Family Psychology, 10*(4), 443-453.

Fantuzzo, J. W., DePaola, L. M., Lambert, L., Martino, T., Anderson, G., & Sutton, S. (1991). Effects of interpersonal violence on the psychological adjustment and competencies of young children. *Journal of Consulting and Clinical Psychology, 59*(2), 258-265.

Feldman, S. E. (1983). Battered women: Psychological correlates of the victimization process. *Dissertation Abstracts International, 44,* 1221-B.

Ferraro, K. J., & Johnson, J. M. (1983). How women experience battering: The process of victimization. *Social Problems, 30,* 325-339.

Follingstad, D. R., & DeHart, D. D. (2000, September). Defining psychological abuse of husbands toward wives: Contexts, behaviors and typologies. *Journal of Interpersonal Violence, 15*(9), 891-920.

Follingstad, D. R., Neckerman, A. P., & Vormbrock, J. (1988). Reactions to victimization and coping strategies of battered women: The ties that bind. *Clinical Psychology Review, 8,* 373-390.

Gay and Lesbian Community Action Council, Minneapolis, MN. (1987). *A Survey of the Twin Cities Gay and Lesbian Community: Northstar Project.* Unpublished manuscript.

Gelles, R. J. (1998). Conjoint therapy for the treatment of partner abuse: Indications and contraindicatations. In A. R. Roberts (Ed.), *Battered Women and Their Families* (pp. 76-97). New York: Springer.

Gelles, R. J., & Straus, M. R. (1989). *Intimate Violence: The Causes and Consequences of Abuse in the American Family.* New York: Simon & Schuster.

Giles-Sims, J. (1983). *Wife Battering: A Systems Theory Approach.* New York: Guilford.

Gondolf, E. (1993). Treating the batterer. In M. Hansen & M. Harway (Eds.), *Battering and Family Therapy: A Feminist Perspective* (pp. 105-118). Newbury Park, CA: Sage.

Goodstein, R. K., & Page, A. W. (1981). Battered wife syndrome: Overview of dynamics and treatment. *American Journal of Psychiatry, 138,* 1036-1044.

Graham-Bermann, S. A. (1998). The impact of woman abuse on children's social development: Research and theoretical perspectives. In G. W. Holden, R. Geffner, & E. N. Jouriles (Eds.), *Children Exposed to Marital Violence* (pp. 21-54). Washington, DC: American Psychological Association.

Greenfeld, L. A., Rand, M. R., Craven, D., Klaus, P. A., Perkins, C. A., Ringel, C., Warchol, G., Maston, C., & Fox, J. A. (1998). *Violence by Intimates: Analysis of Data on Crimes by Current or Former Spouses, Boyfriends, and Girlfriends* (Bureau of Justice Statistics Special Report NCJ 167237). Washington, DC: U.S. Department of Justice.

Groves, B. M. (1999). Mental health services for children who witness domestic violence. *The Future of Children, 9*(3), 122-132.

Grych, J. H., Jouriles, E. N., Swank, P. R., McDonald, R., & Norwood, W. D. (2000). Patterns of adjustment among children of battered women. *Journal of Counseling and Clinical Psychology, 68*(1), 84-94.

Grych, J. H., Seid, M., & Fincham, F. D. (1992). Assessing martial conflict from the child's perspective: The children's perception of interparental conflict scale. *Child Development, 63*, 558-572.

Hanks, S. E., & Rosenbaum, C. P. (1977). Battered women: A study of women who live with violent alcohol-abusing men. *American Journal of Orthopsychiatry, 47*, 291-306.

Hansen, M., & Harway, M. (1993). Directions for future generations of therapists. In M. Hansen & M. Harway (Eds.), *Battering and Family Therapy: A Feminist Perspective* (pp. 227-251). Newbury Park, CA: Sage.

Hansen, M., Harway, M., & Cervantes, N. N. (1991). Therapists' perceptions of severity in cases of family violence. *Violence and Victims, 4*, 275-286.

Hart, B. J. (1993). The legal road to freedom. In M. Hansen & M. Harway (Eds.), *Battering and Family Therapy: A Feminist Perspective* (pp. 13-29). Newbury Park, CA: Sage.

Harway, M., & Evans, K. (1996). Working in groups with men who batter. In M. Andronico (Ed.), *Men in Groups: Insights, Interventions and Psychoeducational Work* (pp. 357-376). Washington, DC: American Psychological Association.

Harway, M., & Hansen, M. (1990). Therapists' recognition of wife battering: Some empirical evidence. *Family Violence Bulletin, 6*, 16-18.

Harway, M., & Hansen, M. (1993a). An overview of domestic violence. In M. Hansen & M. Harway (Eds.), *Battering and Family Therapy: A Feminist Perspective* (pp. 1-12). Newbury Park, CA: Sage.

Harway, M., & Hansen, M. (1993b). Therapist perceptions of family violence. In M. Hansen & M. Harway (Eds.), *Battering and Family Therapy: A Feminist Perspective* (pp. 42-53). Newbury Park, CA: Sage.

Hendricks-Matthews, M. (1982). The battered woman: Is she ready for help? *Social Casework, 63,* 131-137.

Holtzworth-Munroe, A., & Stuart, G. L. (1994). Typologies of male batterers: Three subtypes and the differences among them. *Psychological Bulletin, 116*(3), 476-497.

Holtzworth-Munroe, A., Waltz, J., Jacobson, N. S., Monaco, V., Fehrenbach, P. A., & Gottman, J. M. (1992). Recruiting nonviolent men as control subjects for research on marital violence: How easily can it be done? *Violence and Victims, 7,* 79-88.

Hotaling, G. T., & Sugarman, D. B. (1986). An analysis of risk markers in husband to wife violence: The current state of knowledge. *Violence and Victims, 1,* 101-124.

Hudson, W. W., & McIntosh, S. R. (1981, November). The assessment of spouse abuse: Two quantifiable dimensions. *Journal of Marriage and the Family, 43,* 873-888.

Hughes, H. M. (1982). Brief interventions with children in a battered women's shelter: A model preventive program. *Family Relations, 31,* 495-502.

Hughes, H. M., & Marshall, M. (1995). Advocay for children of battered women. In E. Peled, P. G. Jaffe, & J. L. Edleson (Eds.), *Ending the Cycle of Violence: Community Responses to Children of Battered Women* (pp. 121-146). Thousand Oaks, CA: Sage.

Huth-Bocks, A., Schettini, A., & Shebroe, V. (2001). Group play therapy for preschoolers exposed to domestic violence. *Journal of Child and Adolescent Group Therapy, 11*(1), 19-33.

Jacobson, N. S., Gottman, J. M., Waltz, J., Rushe, R., Babcock, J., & Holtzworth-Munroe, A. (1994). Affect, verbal content and psychophysiology in the argument of couples with a violent husband. *Journal of Consulting and Clinical Psychology, 62,* 982-988.

Jenkins, J. M., Smith, M. A., & Graham, P. J. (1989). Coping with parental quarrels. *Journal of the American Academy of Child and Adolescent Psychiatry, 28,* 182-189.

Jouriles, E. N., McDonald, R., Norwood, W. D., Ware, H. S., Spiller, L. C., & Swank, P. R. (1998). Knives, guns, and interparent violence: Relations with child behavior problems. *Journal of Family Psychology, 12*(2), 178-194.

Jouriles, E. N., Norwood, W. D., McDonald, R., Vincent, J. P., & Mahoney, A. (1996). Physical violence and other forms of martial aggression links with children's behavior problems. *Journal of Family Psychology, 10*(2), 223-234.

Kilpatrick, D. G., Edwards, C. M., & Seymour, A. E. (1992). *Rape in America: A Report to the Nation.* Arlington, VA: National Crime Victims Center.

Koss, M. P. (1990). The women's mental health agenda: Violence against women. *American Psychologist, 45,* 374-380.

Lehmann, P., Rabenstein, S., Duff, J., & Van Meyel, R. (1994). A multi-dimensional model for treating families that have survived mother assault. *Contemporary Family Therapy, 16*(1), 7-23.

Levendosky, A. A., & Graham-Bermann, S. A. (1998). The moderating effects of parenting stress on children's adjustment in woman-abusing families. *Journal of Interpersonal Violence, 13*(3), 383-397.

Levendosky, A. A., & Graham-Bermann, S. A. (2000). Behavioral observations of parenting in battered women. *Journal of Family Psychology, 14*(1), 80-94.

Levendosky, A. A., Huth-Bocks, A., & Semel, M. A. (2002). Adolescent peer relationships and mental health functioning in families with domestic violence. *Journal of Clinical Psychology, 31*(2), 206-218.

Lisak, D., & Roth, S. (1988). Motivational factors in nonincarcerated sexually aggressive men. *Journal of Personality and Social Psychology, 55,* 795-802.

McBurnett, K., Kerckhoff, C., Capasso, L., Pfiffner, L. J., Rathouz, P. J., McCord, M., & Harris, S. M. (2001). Antisocial personality, substance abuse, and exposure to parental violence in males referred for domestic violence. *Violence and Victims, 16*(5), 491-506.

Miller, E. T., & Porter, C. A. (1983). Self-blame in victims of violence. *Journal of Social Issues, 39,* 139-152.

National Coalition of Anti-Violence Programs. (1997). *Anti-Lesbian, Gay, Bisexual and Transgendered Violence in 1996.* New York: Author.

Nutt, R. (1999). Women's gender-role socialization, gender-role conflict and abuse: A review of predisposing factors. In M. Harway & J. M. O'Neil (Eds.), *What Causes Men's Violence Against Women* (pp. 117-134). Newbury Park, CA: Sage.

O'Brien, M., John, R. S., Margolin, G., & Erel, O. (1994). Reliability and diagnostic efficacy of parent's reports regarding children's exposure to marital aggression. *Violence and Victims, 9*(1), 45-62.

O'Hearn, H. G., Margolin, G., & John, R. S. (1997). Mother's and father's reports of children's reactions to naturalistic marital conflict. *Journal of the American Academy of Child and Adolescent Psychiatry, 36*(10), 1366-1373.

Okun, L. (1986). *Woman Abuse: Facts Replacing Myths.* Albany, NY: State University of New York Press.

O'Leary, K. D. (1999, Spring). Psychological abuse: A variable deserving critical attention in domestic violence. *Violence and Victims, 14*(1), 3-23.

O'Leary, K. D., Vivian, D., & Malone, J. (1992). Assessment of physical aggression against women in marriage: The need for multimodal assessment. *Behavioral Assessment, 14*(1), 5-14.

O'Neil, J. M., & Egan, J. (1993). Abuses of power against women: Sexism, gender role conflict, psychological violence. In E. Cook (Ed.), *Women, Relationships and Power: Implications for Counseling* (pp. 49-78). Alexandria, VA: American Counseling Association Press.

O'Neil, J. M., & Nadeau, R. A. (1999). Men's gender-role conflict, defense mechanisms, and self-protective defensive strategies: Explaining men's violence against women from a gender-role socialization perspective. In M. Harway & J. M. O'Neil (Eds.), *What Causes Men's Violence Against Women* (pp. 89-116). Newbury Park, CA: Sage.

Pagelow, M. D. (1989). The incidence of criminal abuse of other family members. In L. Ohlin & M. Tonry (Eds.), *Family Violence* (pp. 263-313). Chicago: University of Chicago Press.

Peled, E. (1998). The experience of living with violence for preadolescent children of battered women. *Youth & Society, 29*(4), 395-430.

Peled, E., & Edleson, J. L. (1995). Process and outcome in small groups for children of battered women. In E. Peled, P. G. Jaffe, & J. L. Edleson (Eds.), *Ending the Cycle of Violence: Community Responses to Children of Battered Women* (pp. 77-96). Thousand Oaks, CA: Sage.

Pence, E. L., & McDonnell, C. (2000). Developing policies and protocols in Duluth, Minnesota. In J. Hanmer & C. Itzin (Eds.), *Home Truths About Domestic Violence: Feminist Influences on Policy and Practice: A Reader* (pp. 249-268). New York: Routledge.

Pillemer, K. A., & Suitor, J. J. (1991). Sharing a residence with an adult child: A cause of psychological distress in the elderly? *American Journal of Orthopsychiatry, 61,* 144-148.

Price, D., & Hansen, M. (1991, August). *Murder/Suicide in Families: Warning Signs for Therapists.* Paper presented at the annual convention of the American Psychological Association, San Francisco, CA.

Prochaska, J. O., & DiClemente, C. C. (1992). The transtheoretical approach. In J. C. Norcross & M. R. Goldfried (Eds.), *Handbook of Psychotherapy Integration* (pp. 300-334). New York: Basic Books.

Pryor, J. (1992). *The Social Psychology of Sexual Harassment: Person and Situation Factors Which Give Rise to Sexual Harassment.* Paper presented at the National Conference on Sex and Power Issues in the Workplace, Washington, DC.

Ramsey-Klawsnik, H. (1993). Interviewing elders for suspected elder abuse: Guidelines and techniques. *Journal of Elder Abuse and Neglect, 5,* 73-90.

Register, E. (1993). Feminism and recovering: Working with the individual woman. In M. Hansen & M. Harway (Eds.), *Battering and Family Therapy: A Feminist Perspective* (pp. 93-104). Newbury Park, CA: Sage.

Renzetti, C. M. (1993). Violence in lesbian relationships. In M. Hansen & M. Harway (Eds.), *Battering and Family Therapy: A Feminist Perspective* (pp. 188-199). Newbury Park, CA: Sage.

Rosenberg, M. S. (1987). Children of battered women: The effects of witnessing violence on their social problem-solving abilities. *The Behavior Therapist, 4,* 85-89.

Rossman, B. B. R. (1994). Children in violent families: Current diagnostic and treatment considerations. *Research and Treatment Issues, 10*(3-4), 29-34.

Segel-Evans, K. (1991). *Safety Self-Control Planning.* Unpublished manuscript.

Segel-Evans, K. (1994, February). *Treatment Issues for Men Who Batter.* Paper presented at the Midwinter Convention of Divisions 29, 42, and 43 of the American Psychological Association, Scottsdale, AZ.

Silverman, J. G., Raj, A., Mucci, L. A., and others. (2001, August). Dating violence against adolescent girls and associated substance use, unhealthy weight control, sexual risk behavior, pregnancy, and suicidality. *Journal of the American Medical Association, 286*(5), 572-579.

Silvern, L., Karyl, J., & Landis, T. Y. (1995). Individual psychotherapy for the traumatized children of abused women. In E. Peled, P. G. Jaffe, & J. L. Edleson (Eds.), *Ending the Cycle of Violence: Community Responses to Children of Battered Women* (pp. 43-76). Thousand Oaks, CA: Sage.

Sonkin, D. J., & Durphy, M. (1989). *Psychological Learning to Live Without Violence: A Handbook for Men.* Volcano, CA: Volcano Press.

Sorenson, S. B., & Bowie, P. (1994). Girls and young women. In L. D. Eron, J. H. Gentry, & P. Schlegel (Eds.), *Reason to Hope: A*

Psychosocial Perspective on Violence & Youth (pp. 167-176). Washington, DC: American Psychological Association.

Spaccarelli, S., Sandler, I. N., & Roosa, M. (1994). History of spouse violence against mother: Correlated risks and unique effects in child mental health. *Journal of Family Violence, 9*(1), 79-98.

Straus, M. A. (1980). The marriage license as hitting license: Evidence from popular culture, law, and social science. In M. A. Straus & G. T. Hotaling (Eds.), *The Social Causes of Husband/Wife Violence* (pp. 39-50). Minneapolis, MN: University Park Press.

Straus, M. A. (1991, September). *Children as Witness to Marital Violence: A Risk Factor for Life-Long Problems Among a Nationally Representative Sample of American Men and Women.* Paper presented at the Ross Roundtable titled "Children and Violence," Washington, DC.

Straus, M. A., & Gelles, R. J. (1988). How violent are American families? Estimates from the National Family Violence Resurvey and other studies. In G. T. Hotaling, D. Finkelhor, J. T. Kirkpatrick, & M. A. Straus (Eds.), *Family Abuse and Its Consequences: New Directions in Research* (pp. 14-36). Newbury Park, CA: Sage.

Straus, M. A., Gelles, R. J., & Steinmetz, S. K. (1980). *Behind Closed Doors: Violence in the American Family.* Garden City, NY: Anchor/ Doubleday.

Tjaden, P., & Thoennes, N. (1998, November). *Prevalence, Incidence, and Consequences of Violence Against Women: Findings From the National Violence Against Women Survey* [Special issue]. Washington, DC: National Institute of Justice and Centers for Disease Control and Prevention Research in Brief.

Tjaden, P., & Thoennes, N. (2000, February). Prevalence and consequences of male-to-female and female-to-male intimate partner violence as measured by the National Violence Against Women Survey. *Violence Against Women, 6*(2), 142-161.

Tomkins, A. J., Mohamed, S., Steinman, M., Macolini, R. M., Kenning, M. K., & Afrank, J. (1994). The plight of children who witness woman battering: Psychological knowledge and policy implications. *Law and Psychology Review, 18*, 137-187.

U.S. Commission on Civil Rights. (1982). *Under the Rule of Thumb: Battered Women and the Administration of Justice.* Washington, DC: U.S. Government Printing Office.

Walker, L. E. A. (1979). *The Battered Woman.* New York: Harper & Row.

Walker, L. E. A. (1984). *The Battered Woman Syndrome.* New York: Springer.

Warshaw, C. (1989, December). Limitations of the medical model in the care of battered women. *Gender and Society, 3,* 506-517.

White, J. W., & Koss, M. P. (1991, Winter). Courtship violence: Incidence in a national sample of higher education students. *Violence and Victims, 6*(4), 247-256.

Williams, K., Umberson, D., & Anderson, K. (2002). Violent behavior: A measure of emotional upset? *Journal of Health and Social Behavior, 43*(2), 189-205.

Wolfe, D. A., & Korsch, B. (1994). Witnessing domestic violence during childhood and adolescence: Implications for pediatric practice. *Pediatrics, 94*(4), 594-599.

Yegidis, B. L. (1989). *Abuse Risk Inventory for Women.* Redwood City, CA: MindGarden.

Yexley, M., Borowsky, I., & Ireland, M. (2002). Correlation between different experiences of intrafamilial physical violence and violent behavior. *Journal of Interpersonal Violence,17*(7), 707-720.

Zuckerman, B., Augustyn, M., Groves, B. M., & Parker, S. (1995). Silent victims revisited: The special case of domestic violence. *Pediatrics, 96*(3), 511-513.

Subject Index

If You Found This Book Useful . . .

You might want to know more about our other titles.

If you would like to receive our latest catalog, please return this form:

Name: _____
                            (Please Print)

Address: _____

Address: _____

City/State/Zip: _____

Telephone: (_____)_____

E-mail: _____

Fax: (_____) _____

I am a:

☐ Psychologist   ☐ Mental Health Counselor
☐ Psychiatrist   ☐ Marriage and Family Therapist
☐ School Psychologist   ☐ Not in Mental Health Field
☐ Clinical Social Worker   ☐ Other: _____

◆   ◆   ◆

Professional Resource Press
P.O. Box 15560
Sarasota, FL 34277-1560

Telephone: 800-443-3364
FAX: 941-343-9201
E-mail: mail@prpress.com
Website: http://www.prpress.com

SA2/01/04

Earn Home Study
Continuing Education Credits*

Professional Resource Exchange, Inc. offers a 6-credit home study continuing education program as a supplement to this book. For information, please return this form, call 1-800-443-3364, fax to 941-343-9201, write to the address below, or visit our website: http://www.prpress.com

*The Professional Resource Exchange, Inc., is approved by the American Psychological Association to offer Continuing Education for psychologists. The Professional Resource Exchange, Inc. maintains responsibility for the program. We are also recognized by the National Board for Certified Counselors to offer continuing education for National Certified Counselors. We adhere to NBCC Continuing Education Guidelines (Provider #5474). Home study CE programs are accepted by most state licensing boards. Please consult your board, however, if you have questions regarding that body's acceptance of structured home study programs offered by APA-approved sponsors. Our programs have also been specifically approved for MFCCs and LCSWs in California and MFTs, LCSWs, MHCs, and psychologists in Florida.

Name: _____
(Please Print)

Address: _____

Address: _____

City/State/Zip: _____
This is ☐ home ☐ office

Telephone: (_____)_____

I am a:

☐ Psychologist   ☐ Mental Health Counselor
☐ Psychiatrist   ☐ Marriage and Family Therapist
☐ School Psychologist   ☐ Not in Mental Health Field
☐ Clinical Social Worker   ☐ Other: _____

Professional Resource Press • P.O. Box 15560
Sarasota, FL 34277-1560

Telephone: 800-443-3364 • Fax: 941-343-9201
E-mail: mail@prpress.com
Website: http://www.prpress.com

SA2/03/05